W9-DBY-734

Industrialization and Developing Countries

Alan Mountjoy graduated from Reading University in 1940 and spent the next six years in the Army. It was during this period, in which he saw service in North Africa, the Middle East and Italy, that he became interested in the problems of the under-developed countries. After the war he was appointed to a junior lectureship in Geography at Bedford College, University of London, where he is now the University Reader. He specializes in the economic and social geography of the Developing World. He has published numerous papers and articles, many being concerned with aspects of the demographic and economic geography of the countries of the Nile basin. He is the author of *The Mezzogiorno* (1973): joint author (with C. Embleton) of *Africa: A Geographical Study* (1970); editor of *Developing the Underdeveloped Countries* (1971) and contributing editor of the 'The Third World' series of articles which appeared in *The Geographical Magazine*, 1973–4. He has been a Visitor to the University of Khartoum and in 1975 was invited to lecture on developing countries' problems at the Universities of Warsaw and Cracow.

Geography editor
Michael Chisholm
Professor of Geography in the
University of Bristol

Industrialization and Developing Countries

Alan B. Mountjoy

Reader in Geography
Bedford College, University of London

Hutchinson of London

Hutchinson & Co (Publishers) Ltd
3 Fitzroy Square, London W1

London Melbourne Sydney Auckland
Wellington Johannesburg and agencies
throughout the world

First published 1963
Reprinted 1964
Second (revised) edition
Reprinted 1968, 1969
Third edition 1971
Fourth (revised) edition 1975

Printed in Great Britain by The Anchor Press Ltd
and bound by Wm Brendon & Son Ltd
both of Tiptree, Essex

ISBN 0 09 123620 7 cased
ISBN 0 09 123621 5 paper

To my wife

Contents

Maps and diagrams   8

Tables   9

Prefaces   10

1 Development and under-development   13

2 The demographic factor: the global setting   27

3 The demographic factor in the under-developed lands   41

4 Industrialization – the panacea?   58

5 Problems of industrialization   76

6 Environmental and human problems   95

7 The form of industrialization   121

8 The progress of industrialization:

  I. Ghana and Nigeria; Chile; Hong Kong   139

9 The progress of industrialization:

  II. India; Egypt   161

10 Conclusion   191

Index   195

Maps and diagrams

1 World per capita net incomes 1970 15
2 World population distribution 1970 33
3 The population cycle 38
4 Age and sex composition, England and Wales
 1881, 1931, 1971 45
5 Age and sex composition, Peru 1961, India 1961,
 Ghana 1960, Egypt, 1960 49
6 The circle of poverty 80
7 World per capita energy consumption *c.* 1970 109
8 World levels of literacy *c.* 1970 116
9 The location of Huachipato 152
10 India's iron and steel industry 166
11 Egypt: industrial establishments by numbers
 employed 1954 185

Tables

1 Estimates of per capita net incomes of selected countries in
  US dollars, 1969–71   18
2 Estimates of world population by continents, 1650–1950   35
3 Expectation of life at birth in selected countries   36
4 Occupational structures of selected countries, 1967–9   61
5 Rates of births, deaths and natural increase for selected
  countries, 1966–70   73
6 Financial aid to developing countries, 1961–71   86
7 Estimated years of supply of important metals   108
8 Per capita energy consumption for selected countries, 1971   111
9 Outlay and investment in India's Five Year Plans,
  1951–74   165
10 India's Five Year Plans (1951–74) by major heads of
   development   165
11 Egypt: industrial and mineral production   182

Preface to the fourth (revised) edition

The United Nations' 'First Development Decade' (1960–9) achieved only moderate success and now, in the middle of the Second Development Decade and looking back on a quarter of a century of efforts at development and their slender results, feelings of disillusionment and uncertainty prevail. The weighty pronouncements of the Club of Rome regarding the finite character of most of our resources and the urgent need for self-discipline and reduction of waste on the part of the developed world; the shock to, and the implications for, both developed and developing economies of the quadrupling of oil prices by the oil-producing states; the need for new thinking on Aid policies; the problems of world-wide inflation, all make the present period one of grave reappraisal. Despite this, or perhaps because of it, there has been a marked expansion of interest in the current problems of the developing world and the need for up-to-date information is greater than ever.

Considerable changes have taken place since this book was first written, and the opportunity has now been taken to make a thorough revision and expansion of the text. In places this has involved rewriting, and throughout statistics have been updated and bibliographies expanded. I record my thanks to Dr D. Hilling, a colleague at Bedford College, for helpful suggestions concerning recent developments in Ghana and Nigeria, and to Miss Valerie Hogg and Miss Barbara Kindell, Departmental Assistants, for their work on the statistical tables and maps. To Mrs Kathryn Dalton, Senior Cartographer, I extend my thanks for the drawing of the new maps.

A.B.M.
August 1974

Preface to the second (revised) edition

It is four years since this book was written, and this period constitutes nearly half the United Nations' 'Development Decade'. Economic development is a dynamic and continuous process and transforms more than economies; thus any work devoted to it must necessarily be revised and brought up to date at frequent intervals. This book has been well received and the occasion of a third printing in the middle of the decade of development seemed an appropriate opportunity to carry out the necessary adjustments and revisions (of major dimensions in the later chapters) in the light of achievements and changes since 1960. The views advanced regarding the place of industrialization within planned development have become substantially endorsed in the last few years, as also has been the emphasis placed upon the demographic and human factors.

The focusing of the world attention upon economic development has, among other things, fostered a great increase in the literature available, and this is reflected in the enlarged bibliographies at the end of each chapter. Also of note has been the establishment in London since 1960 of the Overseas Development Institute, which has already become an authoritative source of information on many aspects of economic development.

A.B.M.
April 1966

Preface to first edition

Since the end of the Second World War governments and peoples in the richer countries of the world have become increasingly aware of the economic problems of their poorer neighbours. It has become an accepted policy of the advanced countries to assist in furthering the development of the human and material resources of these countries. All too often industrialization is regarded uncritically as the cure for the ills of under-development, with its degree of success held to be related simply to the degree of capital investment. Those who offer this prescription are frequently unaware of the multiplicity of problems such policies must overcome and that industrialization is not a universal panacea.

The volume of relevant research and literature is growing, but emanates mainly from economists, sociologists and political scientists; geographers have been slow to make contributions. One reason may be that geographers have been much concerned with a real differentiation within the geography of production whereas the new field directs attention to the geography of consumption and a study of economies. This book aims to focus attention on the complex and interrelated problems – social, economic, political and geographical – that attend development, placing particular emphasis on the problems which accompany attempts at industrialization. The field is broad and much compression has been necessary. No apology is offered for the emphasis on the demographic factor, for this is fundamental to the main problem, as this work tries to show.

I welcome this opportunity to record my thanks to my colleague Miss E. M. Timberlake who read the manuscript and made many constructive criticisms, to the staff of Tate Library, Bedford College, for numerous incidental courtesies, to Miss P. Payne for assistance with the illustrations, and to my wife, who coped cheerfully with the arduous task of typing and assisted with the index.

A.B.M.

1 Development and under-development

In this second half of the twentieth century we have become particularly aware that the world is experiencing a population problem that steadily grows more acute, and also of a growing problem of world poverty. It is not surprising that a broad correlation between these two conditions is readily assumed by large numbers of people, who tend to regard the one as being the prime cause of the other. In fact, this is by no means true, although the demographic factor plays a powerful part in affecting the levels of national wealth and the speed of accumulation of wealth by nations. Much of the poverty of a large part of the world is due to under-development of resources. The United Nations General Assembly recognized this in designating the 1960s as the 'United Nations Development Decade', and the 1970s as the 'Second Development Decade'. In a sense the terms 'under-developed' and 'developing' are euphemisms for 'poor'.

The rich nations of the world are remarkably few in number. They lie in the temperate zone and are populated mainly by European stock. They include the United States and Canada, the United Kingdom and the countries of Western Europe, Australia and New Zealand. The top twenty richest nations include only one-tenth of the world's population. The USSR, Poland, and Ireland might be regarded as well off, and together with the top twenty account for about one-fifth of the world's peoples: four-fifths live in varying degrees of poverty. The poor countries lie mainly in South and Eastern Europe, in Asia, Africa, and Latin America, and their economies are regarded as under-developed in comparison with the few rich lands whose economies reveal a wider diversity of activities embodying the fruits of science and technology and heavy investment of capital.

Under-developed countries are characterized by a high degree of subsistence production with a very limited application of technology; as a consequence manufacturing industry is relatively unimportant and the agricultural sector is paramount. This book is concerned with the development of the industrial sector of such economies as a part of the process of economic development, but it must be understood that industrialization is not a general panacea for all the poor countries of the world. The problem is not simply that their economies lack a substantial industrial sector, but that in many cases even their agricultural sectors are highly inefficient and generally social and institutional patterns make advance in any field extremely difficult. Economic development is not synonymous with industrialization alone, but applies to all sectors of an economy and implies a relative change in their order of importance with the application of science and technology, raising productivity per worker and releasing labour and resources for yet other productive tasks. All sectors (agriculture, mining, manufacturing industry, commerce, services) should advance. Industry, therefore, is but one part of an economy, albeit a very important one, and there is a close interrelationship between all the parts. It is also implicit in the general argument that there is no ceiling to the degree of development possible and that this applies just as much to under-developed countries as to their richer neighbours. Canada, for all its present wealth and degree of development, has vast resources still under-utilized and in this way resembles Brazil and a host of other under-developed lands. Clearly, then, the epithet of 'developed' or 'under-developed' is not based upon potential but rather upon existing levels of wealth and material welfare, but the term 'developing' has a dynamic implication in that it suggests that there is a margin of resources (human and material) that is being developed.

It is not easy to assess and compare the economic welfare of a diversity of nations, particularly when the poorer ones from their very poverty have not the precise knowledge, let alone statistics, of their own conditions. Moreover, it would be hard to get agreement among different peoples as to the meaning of economic well-being: the cultural wants of a highly developed people might seem incomprehensible to the primitive wants for food, clothing and shelter of the world's poorer peoples. On the other hand, some countries generally accepted as under-developed have cultures and civilizations going far back to the time when temperate Western Europe and North America comprised inhospitable forests and bogs. From this it would seem that 'under-developed' is a broad term encompassing states with a wide diversity of attributes and that strictly it should be used to reflect a low standard of technical and economic attainment only.

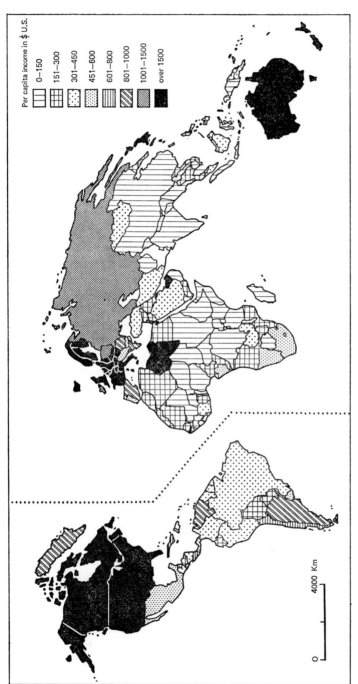

Fig. 1. World per capita net incomes 1970.

Per capita income in $ U.S.

- 0–150
- 151–300
- 301–450
- 451–600
- 601–800
- 801–1000
- 1001–1500
- over 1500

4000 Km

0

The customary common denominator allowing a measure of comparison between countries is that of per capita income, obtained by dividing the estimated total net national income by the total population. The limitations of such a yardstick are apparent if the method of calculation is examined. The net national income is taken to be the sum of all goods and services produced during a year after deduction for fuel, raw materials and all other costs of production including depreciation. Wages, salaries, profits, interest and rent are all included: they are certainly applicable in developed countries but are rather unrealistic for the mass of peasantry in the poorer lands. The difficulty of giving monetary value to peasant production in a subsistence economy is clear, particularly when it is remembered that such peoples perform many services for themselves and neighbours (domestic help, cooking, washing, etc.) which are paid employments in developed countries and appear with some precision in the one reckoning but scarcely at all (or at best as 'guesstimates') in the other. It is likely that subsistence economies are under-valued; also, not only is it difficult to equate local values with world values, but conditions of living have to be taken into account. Minimum requirements of food and clothing are less in hot countries than in areas nearer the Poles and it usually costs less to live in the village than it does in the town, both of which comparisons serve to underline the approximate character of any estimates of net national income and discount the degree of precision that the use of such figures might imply. To this problem may be coupled the frequent lack of knowledge of the size and composition of the working population.

Incomes per head are not the sole indices available; one other that has received some acceptance is a measure of the available energy per head of population. Historically, development has been characterized by a growing replacement of animate by inanimate energy. A country with plenty of power behind the elbows of its workers is one that lives well: productivity in all sections of the economy is high. This productivity may be evaluated in units of currency but it is also measurable in units of energy, for it is generally accepted that a close relationship exists between levels of energy consumption and levels of economic activity (see Table 8, p. 111).[1] Income per head, being expressed in monetary terms, is the more widely accepted, although besides the element of unreliability, a

---

1. Superior figures refer to bibliographical notes at end of chapter.

number of anomalies are patent. For example, the oil-rich sheikdom of Kuwait records a per capita net income nearly twice as high as that of Britain, but it would be ridiculous even to attempt a comparison of the economies of the two countries or the standards of living of the masses of the people in them.

With the help of the table of per capita incomes (Table 1) a map (Fig. 1) has been constructed to show the world distribution of incomes and therefore in broad terms to reveal the rich and poor, the developed and developing nations. An examination of the table and map reveals that the world's wealth is extremely unevenly distributed, that the range between the richest and the poorest nations is surprisingly wide and that on the whole the world is still a very much under-developed planet. The inequality of income between various countries is most striking. A United States citizen nominally commands about twice the per capita income of each of us in the United Kingdom, while our average income per head is ten to fifteen times that of the world's poorest countries. The correlation between highest incomes and the temperate climatic zones is another striking feature and may well reflect climatic influences upon man's mental and physical productivity, a field of study in which much work remains to be done.

Fryer has attempted a classification and analysis of levels of economic development throughout the world. He makes a fourfold division of types of economies: highly developed, semi-developed, under-developed and planned (Communist) economies. The highly developed economy is primarily industrial-commercial, the semi-developed economy is mixed industrial-agricultural. These two groups support about 20 per cent of world population. Under-developed economies are primarily agricultural and may account for 50 per cent of world population, while planned economies exhibit some features from each of the other three groups.[2] This is a useful general classification, but with respect to the under-developed lands needs to be probed further.

DIFFERENCES IN DEVELOPING COUNTRIES

The use of the broad term 'developing' must not blind us to the great differences between the developing countries themselves. Since they comprise the greater part of the world this is hardly surprising, but it is worth drawing attention to these differences to emphazise that there is no omnibus solution to the problems of developing lands, that the final answer for each country is an individual one. Numerous generalizations are frequently made about the developing countries, implying homogeneity rather than heterogeneity. There are some affinities and common characteristics, to be sure, but too often generalizations based upon them mask wide diversities.

By definition one characteristic of the developing countries is

Table 1: *Estimates of per capita net incomes of selected countries, in* US *dollars 1969–71*

US$	US$
Over 4000	*599–500*
USA	Chile, Costa Rica
Sweden	Cuba, Lebanon
3999–2500	*499–400*
Canada, Denmark, W. Germany	Hong Kong, Nicaragua
Kuwait, Norway, Switzerland	Fiji
France, Luxembourg, Netherlands	*399–300*
2499–2000	Brazil, Colombia, Peru
New Zealand, United Kingdom	Guatemala, Turkey, Zambia
Finland, Iceland	Iran, Guyana, Malaysia
1999–1500	*299–200*
Austria, Japan, Italy	Iraq, Jordan, Rhodesia
Libya, Israel	Honduras, El Salvador
1499–1000	Ghana, Ecuador, Philippines
Ireland, Singapore	Morocco, Algeria, Tunisia
USSR, Poland	*199–100*
999–800	Liberia, Egypt, Senegal
	Bolivia, Thailand, Angola
Spain, Greece, Argentina	Mozambique, Kenya, Pakistan
Venezuela	Gambia, Sierra Leone
	Sudan, Uganda
799–700	*Less than 100*
Uruguay, Rep. South Africa	
Malta	Tanzania, Guinea, Indonesia
	India, Zaire, Malawi
699–600	Nigeria, Burma, Mali
Gabon, Trinidad, Portugal	Ethiopia, Afghanistan
Jamaica, Mexico, Barbados	

SOURCE: United Nations, *Statistical Yearbook, 1972*, New York, 1973.

that they are poor, both in income and capital, but there is a considerable range in degrees of poverty. The average net income per head in Burma is less than £30 per annum, in Thailand £75, in Morocco £100, Guyana £130, and so on. At the bottom, poverty is utter and absolute but up the scale it becomes relative and more tolerable. Further, when we examine the conditions of individual countries marked differences are apparent in the distribution of the national income. The per capita figures are averages assuming each man as rich as his neighbour, but this is unreal – even in Communist countries – and in many under-developed countries (e.g. the Middle East oil producers) the bulk of the country's wealth is in the hands of a small minority, the mass of the people existing at a standard far lower than the per capita income implies. Developing countries also differ in their rates of economic growth, some have been making advances while others remain static or even recede.

If we now turn to the population factor it is evident that very important differences materially affecting economies and rates of growth lie in the varying degrees of under- or over-population, the structures of the populations and their rates of increase. Some countries, such as India and Egypt, are heavily over-populated, others, such as Brazil and Ghana, are under-populated; both conditions retard economic development. These demographic features are considered in greater detail later, but here it must be stressed that over-population is but one contributive cause of under-development and national poverty and that only a few countries in the world so far are seriously affected by it. However, the 'population explosions' of the last two decades are especially marked in many under-developed countries, particularly of South-east Asia and Latin America, and their present impoverished economies relying mainly on relatively backward agriculture are unlikely to expand at a rate comparable with the rapid population increase so that low living standards may fall even more.

A further characteristic of developing countries is the substantial part agriculture plays in their way of life. Again wide differences exist, ranging from almost complete dependence upon subsistence agriculture to dependence upon agricultural exports and the imports of some foodstuffs. A capitalization of favourable climate and soil linked with organization and experience has led to specialist commercial production, such as tea in Sri Lanka, cocoa in Ghana, coffee in Brazil, sugar in Cuba, rubber in Malaya; much of this agriculture is highly efficient. Land tenure systems also vary considerably, being tribal or communal in some areas and with individual freeholds in others. In some countries ranked as developing, large-scale irrigation works make natural desert areas habitable and cultivable, in other similarly ranked countries shifting cultivation still pertains. Some developing countries export minerals, oil being the most outstanding example, but also, e.g. copper from Zambia and from Chile, tin from Malaya, iron ore and phosphates from Algeria. It is true to say that the majority of developing countries participate to varying degrees in international trade, exporting usually only one or two primary products, and one of their problems is vulnerability to any fall in world prices.

It will be clear from the foregoing exposition that the developing countries are at widely different stages of advancement. Some, judged by their institutional arrangements, the aptitudes and education of the population and their commercial standing, are ripe for the financial, social and economic changes that development brings; others may be less ready. The readiness of investors, both internal and external, to deploy their capital in a country indicates some measure of its potentiality for advance from a traditional economy to a diversified and complex economic structure and to a position where enough capital is engendered for reinvestment to sustain progress and economic growth.

SOME REASONS FOR UNDER-DEVELOPMENT

Many reasons are advanced to account for under-development. By our present-day standards all countries were once in that condition (although they would not have considered themselves so at the time); what has happened is that over the centuries a few by energy, invention and determination have paced farther and farther ahead of the majority who have moved but slowly, while some have scarcely moved at all. A disturbing feature for the newly awakened world conscience is that the pace of progress of the few leading countries is accelerating rapidly, the progression seems to be geometric – the rich become richer and the poor relatively (and in a few cases, absolutely) poorer. During the years 1952–6 when India had launched her first Five Year Plan her income per head rose by barely £1, whereas Britain's income per head rose by nearly £40. The large rolling snowball picks up much more snow than the tiny one just beginning to roll. This multiplier element, more and more evident as development gets under way, is an integral factor to be invoked in economic plans for development. Cumulative growth, even at apparently slow rates over the years, can, however, have astonishing results. At the beginning of the twentieth century the United Kingdom and the United States enjoyed approximately identical levels of real income per head, but since then the American rate of progress has averaged about 2 per cent and the British about 1 per cent per annum. Seventy years' growth at these speeds and allowing for compound interest now gives the United States rather more than double the British average income per head. The differing rates of growth seem small, but the result over a period of time is of great consequence. Geographers are interested in, and can make useful contributions to, problems of development. A particular field the geographer tends to regard as his own and to evaluate highly in importance is that of resource endowment. There is a danger that the role and significance of possession or non-possession of natural resources in economic development may be misunderstood. Development and under-development is often loosely attributed to the maldistribution of natural resources or to particular geographical disadvantages of certain countries, such as their world position, size, character of the relief, soils and climate. These views are somewhat erroneous; certainly, the possession of varied natural resources can be advantageous but in themselves resources are not decisive. It is not difficult for the geographer to name well-endowed countries that are still backward in development and to indicate other countries, highly advanced yet apparently possessing few natural resources. Brazil and Indonesia, Switzerland and Denmark provide two examples of each. Brazil, despite only limited geological survey, is known to have a plenitude of mineral resources, its large size and varied structure offer a diversity of topography, climates, soils and mineral wealth, yet it remains relatively undeveloped and the per capita income of about £160 is very low. On the other hand, Denmark, despite a lack of minerals and energy resources, a small size, a homogeneity of relief and climate, has developed her economy to such an extent that on a per capita income basis she is one of the richest countries in Europe.

These examples also serve to disprove the contention that size of country is a major factor in development. We can see countries of equal size enjoying a very different standard of living and large countries seem to have no advantage over small ones and vice versa. The multitude of factors bearing upon the well-being of different countries make it very difficult to isolate and evaluate the significance of size in this connection. It is true that great areas may connote a rich and diversified endowment of natural resources, but this merely gives a potentiality. Far more depends upon man's numbers, energy, knowledge, and sense of purpose. Capital can substitute for natural resources as we see in the case of Switzerland where, however, among other geographical factors, position plays an important part.

These examples suggest that much more than possession of resources is necessary for the furtherance of economic development; not even the economist's triumvirate, land (i.e. resources), labour and capital, are by any means the sole determinants of economic progress. Perhaps the most important factors are human ones: in the last resort everything depends upon the people themselves – their numbers and age structures, their enterprise and initiative, their inventiveness, their level of technical knowledge, and above all their desire for material betterment and their willingness to make necessary sacrifices to attain it. Resources in themselves are quite passive: the understanding of their possibilities, the will to use them, the application of capital and technical know-how are the means by which resources become active elements in economies. We must regard the possession of resources as permissive rather than deterministic.

The value and importance of natural resources are not fixed but vary with the stage of development. Spain, for example, by the middle of the nineteenth century was exporting the high-quality, easily won, low-phosphoric-content iron ores of the Viscayan part of Cantabria. In the last decades of the century exports of these ores had risen to an average of five million tons per annum. During the century the ore resources were utilized to earn capital and allowed of capital accumulation. This capital was employed in establishing iron and steel plant on the ore site during the 1880s, and if these development measures had been fully successful, both home and export markets for pig iron and steel might have grown and the ore deposits thus have obtained an enhanced value as an important element in Spain's economic growth. Unfortunately the home market remained remarkably small (there being little comparable development in other branches of the economy) and production costs were too high for successful exports. Moreover, the richer ores rapidly approached exhaustion and probably have only been saved from it by the introduction of the basic steel-making process utilizing phosphoric ores and the open-hearth furnaces utilizing high proportions of scrap, thus reducing the demand for these Spanish ores.

This example of the uncertain beginning of Spain's iron and steel industry serves to demonstrate a number of points. The initial working of the iron-ore deposits on a commercial scale was due to the shrewdness of certain Spaniards and foreigners in appreciating the locational advantages of the deposits situated near the coast, easily accessible to the growing iron industries of Britain and her continental neighbours, and being of high iron content and chemically suitable for the acid Bessemer process. With energy and enterprise capital was raised, much of it foreign, and mining and export companies were formed. The entrepreneurial factor is clearly revealed: the conversion of latent resources into positive wealth awaited those who saw opportunities and were prepared to take risks in order to realize them. Next we see the utilizing of these resources providing a means of capital accumulation (one of the major problems of under-developed countries) and the investment of this capital in industrial plant whereby indirectly the ore resources would act as an accelerator to economic development if other factors of production were favourable. The effect of advances in overseas blast and steel-furnace technology is also noticeable for a fluctuation in demand and a general decline in ore exports (perennial problems of under-developed lands dependent upon markets for one or two primary products). The diminution of export markets underlined the narrowness of the home market for manufactured iron and steel. Whereas capital had been invested in the iron and steel industry there had been little complementary growth in the rest of the Spanish economy and the money to buy the iron and steel products was lacking. The interrelationship between all parts of an economy is thus revealed and raises the question of the effectiveness of development investment that does not take full account of this feature – another major problem of developing countries today.

THE PATH TO DEVELOPMENT

Development involves not merely economic changes but also social and institutional ones, and in many developing countries introduces new sets of values and new concepts of society and government. No path to development is likely to be smooth: the 1848 Chartist disturbances in England and 'year of revolution' in Europe are indicative of the stresses the present developed countries underwent with growing urbanization, the rise of an urban proletariat and the growth in numbers and power of the 'middle class'. In

Europe these social, economic and political changes were spread over the greater part of a century, but the process of adjustment must now be speeded up, for newly developing countries today necessarily plan their economic and social metamorphism in terms of a number of Three, Four or Five Year Plans. One of the difficulties in initiating economic development in many developing countries lies in overcoming institutional opposition. Here, social systems, often based upon concepts of inherited value, are far more rigid than those of Western Europe ever were and severely restrain opportunities for individual advancement. This places more responsibility for economic development upon the government than has been usual in most developed countries where governmental influence has tended to be indirect.

A growing body of economic theory supports the view that economic development is not an inevitable process but must be created and energetically advanced. This may be done by a variety of co-ordinated measures designed to interrupt the free play of social and economic forces. The forces of the market no longer are supreme within developed countries, for both state and private organizations so manipulate conditions that opportunity is more widespread, levels of inequality narrowed and demand influenced. By planned measures of investment, innovation, supports and controls, aggressive policies of economic development are deemed capable of overcoming the stagnation characteristic of many underdeveloped lands. In other words, it is now held that economic development can be induced or even imposed, the goals being determined by governments who become responsible for the co-ordination and planning measures deemed necessary to attain them.[3] These hopeful and stimulating theories are now being proved: in them lies the hope for betterment of four-fifths of the world's population. The next decade will be critical in their application and development.

This broad theory of development is widely held; it is in the precise application that differences emerge, particularly over the degree or priority that developing lands should allow industrialization. Most of the rich countries of the world are highly industrialized and there might seem a case for rapid industrialization in under-developed lands as a short cut to a better standard of living; this view is favoured by Soviet Russia. The previous example of Spain, however, emphasizes the interdependence of the various sectors within an economy and most Western economists favour what has come to be called 'balanced growth' whereby, briefly, agriculture is made more efficient, allowing output per worker to rise, freeing some to move into manufacturing, power, transport and other non-agricultural pursuits. The greater productivity and increasing purchasing power allows of imports and expands the home market for newly manufactured goods. In short, there is an all-round expansion and an upward spiral is created. If these views (expressed here in outline only but elaborated in Chapter 5) are accepted it will be seen that concentration on manufacturing industry offers no short cut to prosperity. The simple outline above fails to take into account demographic factors, widely proving to be the most obstructive of the hindrances to economic development in under-developed countries.

The confidence of economists in their growing understanding of economic forces and their manipulation in this field coincides with the growth of world knowledge of under-development, both by the richer countries and by the under-developed lands themselves. Bodies such as the United Nations, the World Health Organization, the Food and Agricultural Organization, have collected and disseminated facts and figures of world under-development and world poverty. These followed the years of the Second World War in which hundreds of thousands of soldiers from the richer countries saw for themselves the poverty and resignation of many alien lands. The blinkers have slipped from the eyes of people in the few rich countries of the world and the gulf between the internationally rich and poor has been revealed. A world conscience has become manifest as economic inequalities between the rich and the poor increase. The poor also have become far more aware of their poverty as increasing knowledge of higher standards of living in the developed countries has become known, and the desire for change and improvement has begun to be expressed. The sympathy of the richer countries is annually growing in expression by means of technical and financial help and advice, and makes possible the application in under-developed countries of the modern economic theories of development. The pre-war term 'backward countries' is no longer current and by our use in turn of 'under-developed countries', 'less-developed countries' and 'developing countries' we imply the feasibility of development; we assume that with help those countries can do better with their human and material resources. The size of the problem is now tacitly recognized by the acceptance of the term 'Third World' to differentiate the mass of under-developed countries from the 'free world' of the Atlantic bloc and the centrally organized European Communist bloc.

The second half of the twentieth century is seeing for the first time in world history an international onslaught on poverty and backwardness; a new form of pioneering and on an unprecedented scale. In the process not only economies but also societies will become remoulded and whole landscapes may change. Each period of earth history has seemed both exciting and critical to its people, but surely none more so than today.

BIBLIOGRAPHICAL REFERENCES

1. N. B. Guyol, 'Energy Consumption and Economic Development', in N. Ginsburg (Ed.), *Geography and Economic Development* (Chicago, 1960), p. 68.

2. D. W. Fryer, 'World Income and Types of Economies', *Economic Geography* (1958), pp. 283–303.

3. A. Bonné, *Studies in Economic Development* (London, 1957), p. 7.

W. A. Lewis, *The Theory of Economic Growth* (London, 1959).

G. Myrdal, *Economic Theory and Under-developed Regions* (London, 1963).

N. Ginsburg, *Atlas of Economic Development* (Chicago, 1961).

C. Furtado, *Development and Underdevelopment* (Berkeley and Los Angeles, 1964).

A. B. Mountjoy (Ed.), *Developing the Underdeveloped Countries* (London, 1971).

J. Clifford and G. Osmond, *World Development Handbook* (London, 1971).

2 The demographic factor: the global setting

The major problems facing the world today are often thought of as being those posed by the manufacture, possession and threat of nuclear armaments. Yet it would not be right to regard these as of sole paramount importance to humanity at this time. Our greatest problem, the more serious in that we are slow to acknowledge it, is that of excessive population growth in relation to the development of the earth's resources. The world's population problem is not new, but during this century it has become more widely known and its measurement more refined and more complete, thanks to such agencies as the United Nations statistical departments. With this greater and more accurate knowledge has come the realization of the growing seriousness of the problems posed by the rapid increase in human numbers. The manifestation of the problem is growing poverty in certain parts of the world where human increase exceeds that of the development of resources (although it must be appreciated that at the same time in other parts of the world some peoples also increasing in numbers are growing steadily richer). The prospect of the rapid spread and worsening of this situation is before us. The middle years of this century have seen the growth of a social conscience among the better-off nations and greater international co-operation; no longer are eyes closed to the periodic famines that take toll of great populations in South-east Asia.

In any community population numbers, reproductive rate and composition crucially affect the future in that they have a direct influence upon economic development. Here lies the core of the population problem, and that particularly affecting the underdeveloped lands: the relation between population growth and economic development. It is therefore surprising to find that little is yet known with precision about the economics of population. Economists have concentrated more upon the mechanics of economic development with the developed lands as their examples and, more recently, upon the creation of a theory of under-development to aid in the analysis of particular situations. We are yet uncertain, for example, of the effects of over-population, much less the varying rates of population growth, on development. Theories are advanced but they will be tested only as more precise information and statistics become available.

POPULATION THEORY

As is well known, population theory hinges on the law of diminishing returns. Briefly, this law states that, so long as techniques used remain the same, additional application of capital and labour to (e.g.) a given area of land will after a time cause a less than proportionate increase in the output of produce. Industry similarly is subject to diminishing returns, although they can usually be more delayed than in agriculture, since industrial processes are more susceptible of improvements in technique and greater division of labour. In the developed lands the steady increase of population expanding the labour force has led to greater specialization and higher efficiency giving a greater return on each unit of labour. The point of decreasing returns has been avoided by inventions, increases in technical skills and the investment of more and more capital. Unless this happens, from the application of this law, whether in agriculture or manufacturing, after a time we may expect returns to increase by smaller increments until they become constant and then decrease. It follows that there is a point of maximum return, beyond which the application of more capital and labour will not produce proportional returns. It is at this point that a population has reached its optimum or has attained a density which, with given resources and skills, produces the maximum economic welfare or, virtually, the maximum real income per head. It is clear that this concept is highly theoretical if only because it is dealing with a balance between a given people and their resources where numbers, knowledge and skills are constantly changing. The theory, however, does give a definite meaning to the two states of over-population and under-population. With over-population numbers exceed the optimum and with under-population they fall below it; in each case the individual standard of life is lower than it would be if the optimum prevailed.

To put it another way, we may define these conditions as states of society in which there are too many or too few people for the society to live at the highest standard possible with existing land, capital and technical skills. Over-population is a greater drag on economic expansion than under-population and the most serious problem-areas in the world today are those over-populated but under-developed; here further population increases depress living conditions still more. It is salutary to view the world's population problem not as one of numbers but of standards of living. It is true that population expansion was a vital and dynamic factor in the economic development of nineteenth-century Britain, but here, via a technical revolution in agriculture, was burgeoning an industrial economy where decreasing returns were prevented by the investment and ploughing back of more and more capital, by increasing specialization and steadily developing technical processes and skills. A different state of affairs evolved in South-east Asia, although with fewer records it is less satisfactorily explained. One reason may be the very antiquity of these civilizations in the great fertile river basins, where slow improvements and developments in agriculture took place over a long period, for a time no doubt keeping pace with slow population growth. The west European environment was conducive to movement, intercourse and trade, to the mining and working of metals, and it created by the end of the sixteenth century a class of persons removed from the land, a money economy, such far-reaching institutions as the joint stock company, and supported an agrarian revolution that opened the way to full industrialization with its harnessing and application of mechanical energy. In South-east Asia the more static agrarian way of life offered less scope for technical advances and division of labour, and the predominantly subsistence economy prevented the generation of much capital. Thus these traditional ways persisted and the onset of decreasing returns was not withstood. Standards of living fell acutely with the heavy population increases of more recent times, which now bleed the economies with their absorption of capital, inflate the problem by their very immensity and impede the belated take-off to a more balanced and productive economy.

The heavy drag of high rates of population increase upon economic development is frequently underestimated. Each new member of society raises the bill for education, health and other public services and the provision of employment for him increases the demand for capital investment. A rate of population increase of $1\frac{1}{2}$ per cent per annum requires at least a 2 per cent per annum increase in output if the standard of living is to grow at all. This is a substantial task needing capital investment of 8–10 per cent of the national income, whereas most under-developed countries save only about 5 per cent of the national income. In fact, this rate of development would be comparatively modest and would take over 100 years to double the standard of living. Also, rates of population increase in most of the developing lands are in excess of $1\frac{1}{2}$ per cent per annum: rates of $2\frac{1}{2}$ and 3 per cent per annum are now being recorded, requiring a capital investment of 10–12 per cent of the national income even to hold the present low living standards. In 1951 United Nations experts estimated that reasonably fast development of agriculture and industry in these lands would require an investment of $19 134 million every year.[1] Rates of population increase have continued to rise since then, so it seems that even this tremendous figure is likely to be an under-estimate. Thus the heavy task of finding the means for the raising of output is made more herculean the greater the rate of population increase. Past experience suggests, however, that once standards of living are raised birth rates tend to fall.

This discussion would be incomplete if opposing views were not cited. The above Malthusian view, widely accepted, is challenged by those who feel that population pressure serves to stimulate innovation, and that since savings are mainly accumulated by the young, a rapidly growing and therefore youthful population should have a high rate of capital accumulation and therefore of investment. These views, connected with such names as Adam Smith and Marx, derive mainly from studies of developed rather than under-developed economies.

THE GROWTH OF WORLD POPULATION

There is a great body of literature discussing the varied aspects of the world's population problem and it is not intended here to present more than an outline to serve as a frame for a more detailed consideration of the place, problems and possibilities of industrialization.[2] In these matters the demographic factor carries great weight for the population element underlies and colours the whole economic scene. It would be wrong, however, to ascribe development or under-development simply to the weight of the population force, particularly under- or over-population. Development is the result of the interaction over considerable periods of time of many interdependent factors, mutually cumulative in their effects; there is no simple basic factor. The often quoted 'economic factor' – a compound of capital, land and labour – is only one of the ingredients, and non-economic factors also play quite decisive roles including for example the physical and mental character of a people in addition to their numbers, sex ratios and rates of increase; geographical position may even carry more weight than resource endowment and much may depend on the prevailing social and political organization. If this were not the case national poverty could be said to rest wholly on physical circumstances beyond human control.

A review of the present situation of world population and its recent history serves to underline its dynamic character. Each day changes take place; population is in constant transition. Census coverage and information are constantly improving but still the great majority of peoples in under-developed countries are not adequately enumerated and the more detailed information, such as age groupings in relation to births and deaths (very necessary in estimating population growth), is rarely available. The margin of error in the United Nations' estimate of world population may be as high as 5 per cent.

The United Nations' *Demographic Yearbook* gives the population of the world in 1971 as 3706 million.[3] The present annual increment to this stupendous figure is of the order of eighty million or much more than the population of the United Kingdom. The population of the world in 1900 has been estimated at about 1550 million and this suggests that world population has doubled during the past sixty years. The fact that world population increased by about 500 million in the first half of this period (1930 total 2013 million) and by over 1000 million during the last thirty years makes abundantly clear the multiplying factor that is so alarming in population increase. Not only do the absolute numbers grow steadily, but the rate of increase itself increases. The annual rate of increase is now estimated at 2 per cent and this must be regarded as a compound interest rate. Huxley estimates the rate of increase in 1650 at 0·5 per cent; it did not reach 1 per cent until well into the present century; twenty years ago it was 1·3 per cent. This acceleration in the rate of increase is continuing and may well do so for at least the next two or three decades. 'Population increase proceeds . . . by acceleration, and the result has been to convert an early state of virtual stability into one of slow but appreciable growth, then into rapid expansion, and finally into an explosive process.'[4] At a rate of increase of 0·5 per cent per annum the population will double itself in approximately 140 years; at 1 per cent in seventy years; 1·5 per cent in forty-seven years and 2·0 per cent, which we have now reached, in thirty-five years. We may expect the staggering total of 7000 million by the year 2000 if the present trend continues. The problem of feeding, clothing and occupying this mass of humanity must be solved in the lifetime of children already born. The longer we dawdle, the more intractable the problem we bequeath them.

The map (Fig. 2) displays the very uneven distribution of man on the earth and reveals three principal agglomerations of population, in Europe, in eastern North America and in South-east and eastern Asia. The character of the earth's surface and the climate help to determine the distribution of man and to a large extent account for the crowding into a small number of favoured but limited areas, although the degree of development and character of the economy play their part, particularly in accounting for local variations within the main areas. Both the European and North American populous areas lie in the zone of cyclonic weather, alleged to favour the greatest mental and physical well-being, whereas the Asian population centres are in the monsoonal zone, where the conjunction of moisture and warmth makes possible the production of abundant food per acre. In these three main areas 2000 million people crowd into about four million square miles – an area slightly greater than that of Canada or a third larger than Australia and under half the size of the USSR. It seems, further, that three-quarters of the world's population lives on no more than a twelfth of the earth's land surface, giving a density of 500 per sq. mile. The wealthier industrial nations are able to draw upon considerable food supplies from more sparsely peopled areas, but the densely peopled agricultural lands lack the wealth to do this and their increasing numbers press directly upon the means of subsistence, usually engendering conditions of extreme poverty. It is notable that more than half the population of the world lives in Asia and that this proportion is steadily increasing.

Rates of increase vary markedly but are generally high among the developing lands and moderate or low in richer countries (Table 5, p. 73). Thus whereas at the beginning of this century there was one European for every two Asians, by the end of the century this ratio may have become one to four. One of the features of the next few decades will be a continuous decline in the relative importance of Europe, including the USSR. It seems likely that by the year 2000 the present population of Africa (310 million) will have increased nearly two and a half times; that of Asia (1820 million) by nearly

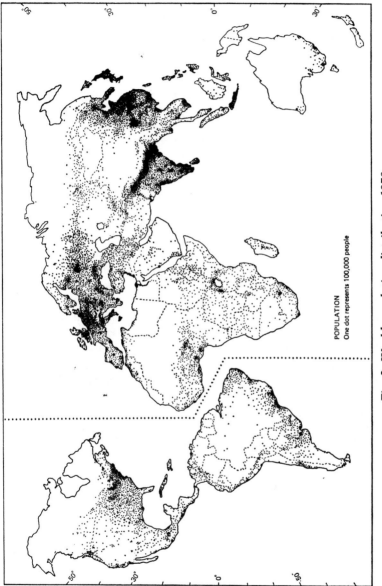

POPULATION
One dot represents 100,000 people

Fig. 2. World population distribution 1970.

three times and that of Latin America (300 million) by over three times. The rest of the world population will increase by a little less than three-quarters of its present level. It will be seen that this growth is proportionately greatest in the regions of low standards of living. It would seem that we have now entered the most explosive period of population growth from which the richer and developed countries can no longer be insulated. The year 2000 is relatively close (it is not so far ahead as the end of the Second World War is behind us) and since the problems become more acute with each year that passes it would seem that the next decade may be one of the most critical in human history.

THE HISTORY OF POPULATION GROWTH

It is probably well realized now that the very great population increases during this century, and particularly since the close of the Second World War, are not the result of an increase in human fertility, but rather of a decline in mortality resulting from advances in, and the wider application of, modern medicine. It is striking to realize that whereas it has taken the world 200 000 years to attain a population of 2500 million, it will now only require thirty years to add a further 2000 million. Of course, our reasonably precise knowledge of the size of the world's population goes back barely two centuries. The farther we go back in time the more we must rely on guesswork and the more flimsy the evidence upon which these guesses can be based. It is clear that for at least 10 000 years there has been a steady increase in world population; temporary decreases or stagnation may have occurred here and there but the trend has been persistently upward. Some 10 000 years ago, during the hunting stage of man's existence, world population is thought to have been between five and ten million; 3000 years later, with the onset of civilization, the figure may have risen to twenty million. A progressive increase of numbers followed with development in agriculture, trade and manufacture and at the time of Christ world population may have been about 150 million.[5] By the middle of the seventeenth century, when estimates are more certain, this figure had reached approximately 550 million. Seventeen centuries gave a four-fold world population increase but the past three centuries have seen that population multiply itself five times. Thus it seems that the modern phase of accelerating population increase began during the seventeenth century and was well under way in the eighteenth century.

The sharp upward turn in the rate of population increase during this period may be related to the striking advances made in the fields of agriculture, industry, medicine and sanitation. In these the countries of Western Europe were in the forefront. Between 1650 and 1900 Europe's population, despite considerable emigration, multiplied itself four times and its share of the world's population increased from 22 to 27 per cent (Table 2). Asia's population grew at a slower rate and by 1900 the increase was about three times. By the end of the first half of this century Europe's population had increased almost six-fold since 1650 and Asia's population had quintupled. Thus the rate of Asia's population increase has gone up appreciably during this century. Admittedly, higher rates of increase since the seventeenth century have been recorded in the relatively empty lands of the Americas, but the numbers involved have been relatively small; four-fifths of world population is now in Europe and Asia.

Table 2: *Estimates of world population by continents, 1650–1950*

	(*Millions*)									
	1650	%	*1750*	%	*1850*	%	*1900*	%	*1950*	%
Europe	103	22·0	144	21·0	274	25·2	423	27·0	574	23·0
North America	1	0·2	1	0·1	26	2·5	81	6·0	168	7·0
Latin America	7	1·4	10	1·4	33	3·0	63	4·0	163	6·5
Africa	100	21·3	100	14·3	100	9·1	120	7·7	199	8·0
Asia	257	54·7	437	63·0	656	60·1	857	55·0	1376	55·0
Oceania	2	0·4	2	0·2	2	0·1	6	0·3	13	0·5
World Total	470	100	694	100	1091	100	1550	100	2493	100

SOURCES: W. F. Willcox, *Studies in American Demography*, New York, 1940 (for 1650–1900).
United Nations, *Demographic Yearbook, 1958* (for 1950).

Although there is reason to believe that the population of Japan and China began increasing more rapidly during the latter part of the seventeenth century (i.e. before the substantial advance in Europe began) on the whole the rise in the rate of increase of Asia's population came after that of Europe, becoming noticeable during the nineteenth century as a result of European influence. It would seem that in certain respects the great increases of population in Asian countries in the recent decades might be regarded as a repetition of a pattern already passed through in Europe. There are grave differences, however, particularly in the speed of occurrence and the magnitude of the populations undergoing them.

The period of really critical increase in the rate of population growth has been the last three decades. Until 1940 the world's annual increase of population was 1·0 to 1·2 per cent. This quickening in the rate of growth has not yet been checked, the situation will worsen before we can hope for easement. This recent excessive acceleration has been due to a series of scientific and medical advances whose application has resulted in what has been termed 'death control'. The vigorous introduction of medical services, new drugs, instruction in hygiene and improved sanitation into the poorer countries has often markedly extended the expectation of life. In Britain the expectation of life at birth is about 70 years, in India at the beginning of the century it was only 24, but by 1960 it had increased to 41 years (Table 3). Postponement of death has been

Table 3: *Expectation of life at birth in selected countries*

	(*Years*)				
	1900	1930	1950	1960	1970
United Kingdom	52	—	69	71	71
France	47	—	65	70	72
Bulgaria	40	46	—	66	71
Japan	44	—	58	70	72
India	24	27	32	41	—
Chile	—	37·5	52	57	—
Mexico	—	33	—	57	62
Kenya	—	—	—	—	44
Egypt	—	—	—	53	—

The average of male and female life expectations is given.
SOURCES: United Nations, *Demographic Yearbook, 1953*, Table 19; *1958*, Table 31; *1964*, Table 23; *1971*, Table 3.

particularly successful in the case of infants, and infant mortality rates in the under-developed countries have started to show astonishing reductions. During the period 1948–67 Sri Lanka's mortality rate fell from 92 to 48 and Chile's from 147 to 92 deaths under the age of 1 year per thousand live births – examples typical of most of the under-developed countries.

The result of all this has been that the death rate has been falling exceptionally fast in many under-developed countries of Latin America and Asia and is beginning to fall in Africa, whereas no appreciable fall has yet occurred in their birth rates. We find that high death rates of, say, 30 per thousand have been halved without any corresponding diminution of birth rates of the order of 40 per thousand. It may not be wise to press analogies with Europe too far in these matters, but it is worth noting that there was a considerable time lag in Western Europe (half a century in fact) before a decline in birth rates followed the fall in death rates. The people of Western Europe during the last two and a half centuries have been influenced by four social and economic movements: so-called revolutions in agriculture, industry, medicine and sanitation, and birth control. Analysis of the resultant pattern of population reaction to these movements helped in the formulation of what is conveniently known as the population cycle or the demographic transition.

THE POPULATION CYCLE

As a result of social and economic developments populations usually pass through a number of distinct stages in their growth. In the pre-scientific period both birth and death rates were high: population increase was slow and irregular. This period is known as the 'high fluctuating' stage and in this country was coming to an end early in the eighteenth century. As medical knowledge and sanitation improved, the next phase occurred: the 'early expanding' phase of rapid increase. In this stage death rates fall markedly but birth rates remain both high and constant and a maximum increase of population occurs. The third or 'late expanding' stage finds death rates continuing their fall, but, responsive to rising standards of living, families become smaller and a sharp decline in the birth rate sets in: population still increases, but at a less rapid rate. Finally in the 'low fluctuating' phase, both birth and death rates steady at a low level (in Britain at about 16 and 12 per thousand respectively), increase still takes place, but very slowly and the population seems to be reaching a phase of stabilization. These conditions for England and Wales are demonstrated in Fig. 3.

It may well be thought that the developing lands currently receiving the benefits of advanced agriculture, industry and medicine are now passing through the early stages of the population cycle and that a pattern similar to that of Western Europe will ensue. However, the problems of these countries, and indeed the world's population problem as a whole, arise from the very different timing and tele-scoping of the various phases.

First, it must be realized that in Western Europe, the type area,

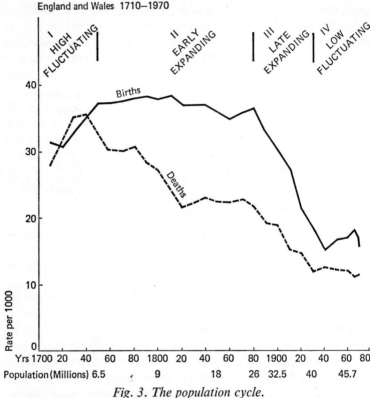

Fig. 3. The population cycle.

change was gradual. The knowledge and application of death control arose from a long period of trial and error. The slow but steady accretion of population both stimulated and allowed full advantage to be taken of the new developments in industry and transport: in short, they permitted economic expansion which throughout the nineteenth century raised standards of living, making possible, at a price, the choice of comforts and amenities and thus fostering a material desire to limit families. In England and Wales this had started to take effect in the decade 1871–80, when the birth rate, dropping from 35·5 to 34·1, started a downward plunge that was not arrested until during the Second World War. The situation is very different in the developing countries where Europe's hard-won knowledge of two centuries is readily, and relatively instantaneously, available. In the reduction of death rates what has taken Western Europe two centuries to accomplish is now occurring in one or two decades in parts of Asia and Latin America. This is graphically illustrated by the much-quoted example of Sri Lanka, where DDT and a well-organized campaign wiped out the malarial mosquito in seven years (1945–52) and the death rate fell from 22 to 10 per thousand. It took about 300 years to clear malaria from England and the comparable fall in the death rate was spread over seventy years. During this time, however, England's birth rate fell from 35 to 15 per thousand whereas that of Sri Lanka remains above 30 and the population is increasing at a rate that will double it in thirty years. Here is the explanation of the population explosion now becoming manifest: birth rates still in stage 2 of the population cycle, out of phase with falling death rates often already approaching stage 4.

These are fundamental differences from the population cycle of Western Europe and it is possible that a new cycle applicable to the developing lands will be formulated. These differences are particularly manifest in the structure of these populations and in the character of the economic development they must necessarily engender. Development, particularly industrial development, will not be an evolution from within (as in Western Europe), but will be a rapid imposition from without. The scale of development, too, must be very different since the initial populations are more vast and their standards of living lower than those of Western Europe two centuries ago, and the greater these populations the greater the rate of growth of total output needed to raise the standard of living.

BIBLIOGRAPHICAL REFERENCES

1. United Nations' Dept. of Economic Affairs, *Measures for the Economic Development of Under-developed Countries* (New York, 1951).

2. Political and Economic Planning (PEP), *World Population and Resources* (London, 1955) and United Nations, *The Future Growth of World Population* (New York, 1958).

3. United Nations, *Demographic Yearbook 1972* (New York, 1973).

4. J. Huxley, 'Population and Human Fulfilment', essay in *New Bottles for New Wine* (London, 1957), p. 174.

5. J. Huxley, 'Population and Human Destiny', *World Review* (1950), pp. 7–8.

D. L. Linton, 'Population and Food in the Tropical World', *The Advancement of Science* (1961), pp. 391–401.

C. Clark, *Population Growth and Land Use* (London, 1967).

J. I. Clarke, 'World population and food resources: a critique', Inst. Brit. Geogs. *Special Publication, No. 1*, (1968), pp. 53–70.

3 The demographic factor in the under-developed lands

AGE STRUCTURES

The dynamic character of population growth and its portents have been outlined; it is now necessary to examine, with particular reference to the developing lands, those aspects of population that leave the greatest impress upon a country's economy. The age structure of a population is a factor of the greatest demographic and economic weight. In the first place age distribution conditions birth and death rates in a community while being itself, of course, an intimate expression of them; or in other words, future population growth is related to past trends because of their expression in the age structure. Crude birth rates are expressed as per thousand of the total population, but it is an important refinement to consider the ratio of numbers of births to numbers of women in the reproductive cycle (ages 15–45). Variation in the proportions of women in these age groups will alter the birth rate, assuming that the number of children produced by each woman (fertility) remains the same. Actual age distribution within these (the reproductive cycle) age groups is also important. Women approaching the end of their reproductive period are less fertile than younger women, thus a change in the age distribution of women aged 15–45 will also affect the birth rate: if relatively more women appear in the age group 20–24 than before, other things being equal, the birth rate rises.

The proportion of women of child-bearing age to the whole community varies markedly in countries at different stages of the population cycle, implying that some populations are far more fecund than others. Stage 4 populations, for example, are far 'older' than those in earlier stages. In such analyses birth rates related to the specific ages of mothers are valuable but it is very rare for such age-specific birth rates of under-developed lands to be known, consequently one can only examine the patterns in the developed lands, where statistics are available, and in broad terms transpose the resultant trends to assume similar patterns in the developing communities. This relies upon the expectation that future structure of certain populations will resemble the past structure of others.

Death control, that has become so marked a feature in developed lands during the past two or three decades, has the effect of prolonging the lives of some older people. They are less productive but nevertheless need food and shelter, but while enlarging the total population have virtually no effect upon the birth rate and population trend. The main result of death control is, however, a reduction of the crude death rate by a lowering of infant mortality. Children thus saved in infancy are likely to live out an appreciable lifetime, and thus far more female children will reach child-bearing age and in turn increase the number of babies produced for any given crude birth rate. This is a significant feature that suggests there can be little hope of rapid reduction in population increase in these lands, for even when crude birth rates start to fall, for an appreciable time the large numbers bearing children will cause an absolute increase in numbers born. It is true that the fall in the infant mortality rate is far faster than it was in Western Europe and there is some hope that when birth rates do fall in the developing lands they also will drop far more rapidly than they did in the developed countries.

Once the numbers of births decline the age structure of a population will slowly change. The survivors of the former high birth rates become older and pass out of the child-bearing period, to be replaced only partially by the succeeding generations. This was the pattern exhibited by many west European countries immediately prior to the Second World War. In England and Wales the percentage of people of 45 and over in 1881 was just under 20, by 1931 it had risen to 31 per cent, and in 1971 was 37 per cent. Such marked changes in a population's age composition are reflected in a changing rate of increase and affect the degree to which a population is reproducing itself. Differences between crude birth and death rates are inadequate for determining rate of replacement, since a population may still be increasing even when the mothers of a generation are not replacing themselves. The experience of the United Kingdom again demonstrates this. Between 1923 and 1946 our net reproduction rate was below 1·0 (the exact replacement rate), but our population continued to grow because there were large numbers of people born earlier when both the birth rate and number of births per annum were much higher. These people, being both in and after the reproductive age groups but still some way from death, retard the effects of incomplete replacement. However, the use of the measure known as the net reproduction rate clarifies the situation. Here age-specific birth rates of female children are adjusted with similar age-specific death rates and expressed as a proportion of that necessary to maintain a stationary population: in other words it is a measure of how far mothers are reproducing themselves. A rate of 1·0 means that a generation of women of child-bearing age is exactly reproducing itself. During the 1930s the net reproduction rate of England and Wales was barely 0·8, which signified that every ten women of child-bearing age left after them only eight daughters. If such a rate persisted over several generations the total population would level off and then begin to decline.

Other factors affecting birth rates and related usually to social and economic conditions are the marriage rate, the age of marriage, and birth control. Here again data are increasingly available for developed countries but as yet scarcely known for the lesser-developed lands. It is sufficient here to notice that subject to certain provisos the greater the marriage rate (i.e. the number of persons married per thousand of the population) the greater the fertility to be expected of a population and, since younger women are more fertile than older women, a lowering of the average age of marriage may well lead to a rise in the crude birth rate. An underlying assumption here is that illegitimate births form but a very small proportion of total births. If the employment of birth control increases and becomes more effective, then a fall in the birth rate is to be expected. This feature, related to under-developed countries, will be discussed in more detail later.

These examples have been mentioned to demonstrate how the vital processes within the framework of the particular stage in the population cycle affect, and in turn are affected by, the age structure of a population. Such structure can reflect the relevant stage in the population cycle and in broad terms can indicate expanding or contracting populations in the years ahead, always assuming, of course, that existing birth and death rates persist. In turn economic reactions differ in expanding and contracting societies: the long-term requirements of a predominantly young and vigorous population will bear little resemblance to those where half of the population is over 40.

THE AGE AND SEX PYRAMID

The examination of the age and sex structure of populations is as necessary a task for the geographer in his interpretation of the human geography as it is for the economist and social scientist concerned with more specific aspects of the economy and its parent society. No examination of the problems of the developing lands can be real or complete without such a study. The most widely used device for illustrating this information is the age and sex pyramid, whereby the information is graphed so that the essential character of the population structure may be clearly seen and the population history readily interpreted. The graph comprises a central vertical scale of age groupings, usually employing five-year groupings with the youngest group, 0–4, at the bottom. The percentage that each of these groups forms of the entire population is plotted on a horizontal scale, males being placed to the left of the vertical scale and females to the right of it. Actual numbers may be plotted horizontally, but this is often less useful than percentages since neither proportions nor comparisons are so easily read off. The graph represents the total population, and its characteristically triangular shape stems from the normally diminishing proportion of males and females in each successively older age group. Such a graph covers nearly a century and reflects the diverse experience of the given society: epidemics, wars, migrations, economic recessions, the advances of medicine are all mirrored in the vital processes and appear on the graph. In turn, these features, resembling gashes and scars on an idealized outline, over the years will ascend the scale, contract and vanish and in this sense the document in addition to information of the past and the present can give a partial, but valuable, picture of the future.

A brief examination of the age and sex pyramids for England and Wales in 1881, 1931 and 1971 will demonstrate many of these points (Fig. 4). The graph for 1881 is markedly different in shape from the other two and records the age structure at the close of the early expanding stage in Britain's population cycle. A high and steady birth rate related to a steadily diminishing death rate had engendered a rapid increase of population, each succeeding five-year age group has outnumbered its predecessors and a steadily increasing specific mortality rate tapers off the pyramid fairly regularly. This population, in 1881, is basically 'young', some 60 per cent of the population being less than 30 years old. The period covered by the

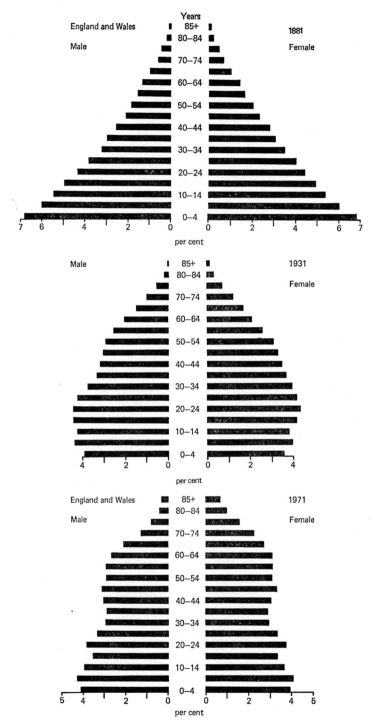

Fig. 4. Age and sex composition, England and Wales 1881, 1931, 1971.

graph is free from major wars but did see a considerable loss of population by emigration, helping to account for a slight steepening in the adult portion of the graph.

In 1931 a very different picture is presented. This graph records the structure of the population at the end of the late expanding stage in its population cycle. Death rates have continued to fall but birth rates have fallen even more sharply. This results in a pyramid with a narrowed base where succeeding five-year age groups are smaller than their predecessors. A greater expectation of life is indicated by a rather higher proportion in the uppermost age groups, and a thickening in the 15–30-year groups is suggestive of the ageing population that is to come. The effect of the First World War may be seen in the reduction in the proportions of males in 35–50-year age-bracket and is a contributive cause of the smaller proportion of children in the 5–10-year-old groups. The shape this pyramid assumes shows that the population is growing older in the sense that the most numerous in it are no longer children but the younger adults.

The tendency for a contraction in the lower age groups was continued through the 1930s. Smaller families had become fashionable, partly as a result of the economic depression and also a desire for increasing amenities – satirized at the time as a preference for the baby Austin rather than the baby. This reduction in fertility from 1881 was brought about mainly by the acceptance and increasing practice of birth control. The result, seen in the third pyramid, was a marked undercutting of the base until the Second World War (this was the period when the net reproduction rate dropped as low as 0·78). There followed the sharp rise in births that characterized the early post-war years and the emergence of the 'welfare state'. The population has aged further, producing a firm 'middle-aged spread', but the numbers to sustain this burden in the coming years have once more grown. Much more could be gleaned from these three pyramids, but it is irrelevant to the present discussion. An important point that emerges is that the various stages of the population cycle create characteristic pyramids by which they may be recognized.

The difference in outline between populations in the early expanding (stage 2) and the late fluctuating (stage 4) phases of the cycle is striking. The rather squat, broad-based figure contrasts with the taller, more bulbous and pedestalled shape. Pyramids for England and Wales in 1881 and 1971 are good examples. Between them in the late expanding (stage 3) phase the rapidly falling birth rate and still declining death rate is reflected in a narrower base and rather taller structure than for stage 2. The 1921 pyramid for England and Wales (with the effects of the First World War discounted) would serve as an example. Whether, after oscillating through the low fluctuating phase (stage 4) population will settle into a fifth, or stationary, stage we have yet to discover.

A close correlation is discernible between those countries experiencing stage 1 and 2 of the cycle and those countries with the lowest per capita income. Little statistical data are yet available for the majority of stage 1 countries (mainly in Africa), but it is reasonable to expect that they in turn will enter, or are already entering, stage 2 as their high death rates become reduced.

JUVENILITY

Age and sex pyramids for four countries in the early expanding (stage 2) phase (Peru, India, Ghana and Egypt) are plotted in Fig. 5 and may be taken as typical. It will be seen that their outlines are remarkably similar. All show the characteristic broad base resulting from high birth rates associated with a low or very low death rate. Each of these countries has a crude birth rate around 40 per thousand of the population but only Ghana and India exhibit typical late (stage 2) death rates (21 per thousand). The other three now have death rates resembling those in stages 3 and 4 in Europe (Egypt 15 and Peru 12 per thousand), illustrative of the success of death control and the telescoping of a part of the European-type population cycle. The effect of these very low death rates of recent years is to be seen in the exceptionally high proportion of young children, for well over 40 per cent of their populations were under 15 years of age during the early 1960s. It is to be noted that in the 1970s, when the bulk of these children have entered the reproductive period, such populations will be of unprecedented fecundity. The fact that youth represents so high a proportion of the total population is also a reflection of the rather low expectation of life in these countries. The pyramids are far more squat than those for west European countries and it will be seen that the proportion of these populations attaining 65 years and over is very small, averaging 3 to 4 per cent, whereas 11 per cent is more typical of Western Europe. However, expectation of life in these countries is rising quickly (Table 3):

future years will see larger absolute numbers reaching the top of the pyramid, although the proportion of the total population may still be quite small.

These features have economic as well as demographic significance. First, it is clear that juvenility is a prominent characteristic of the majority of the population of developing lands since the proportion of population below 15 years of age is of the order of 40–45 per cent. The selection of the fifteenth year is clear cut in the case of the developed lands, for the demands of full-time education up to that age prevent the individual from entering full-time employment. This is far less so in less-developed lands where end-of-school age may well be lower and where school attendance is less obligatory (in fact, if not in law). However, age-group statistics are usually expressed in five-year intervals and there is little doubt that children below 15 years of age should not be regarded as fully productive members of society. Consequently it is felt that a classification into age groups, 0–14, 15–64 and over 65 generally has economic significance in both developed and developing countries. The selection of 0–19 as a first grouping, while revealing that over half the population of under-developed lands are usually children and adolescents, has less economic although much social significance.

The large number of children of low or negligible productivity in these stage 2 countries is a great burden on the economy. They and the smaller proportion of old folk must be supported mainly by the productivity of the remaining adult population. Their numbers related to the active population (15–64 years) give a 'dependency ratio'. It is not always appreciated that owing to the age structure the proportion of adults (15–64 years) to the whole population is generally smaller than in developed lands (e.g. England and Wales 62 per cent, but Peru 53 per cent in 1957). Married couples the world over know that the principal expenditure within a family is on the children, to provide them with food, clothes and housing. Where families are big and incomes low there is little expenditure possible on non-essentials and amenities: standards remain low. With a rapidly increasing population the demand on investment merely to maintain basic living standards will be very great and economic development correspondingly is slowed down.

The degree of return on capital invested may be expressed as the capital: output ratio or capital coefficient. This is a measure of the number of units of net capital investment required to increase the value of output by one unit per annum. Returns on investment vary

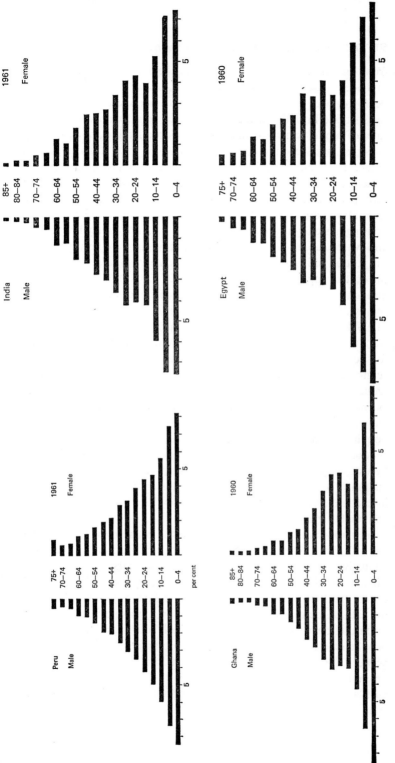

Fig. 5. Age and sex composition, Peru 1961, India 1961, Ghana 1960, Egypt 1960.

from one undertaking to another and the ratio is a guiding figure in the selection of projects for investment and in the most economical deployment of investment capital. The higher the ratio the smaller the increase in national income and vice versa. Our knowledge of rates of capital formation in under-developed lands is, however, very imperfect and here the coefficient can be no more than a general guide.[1] Each individual in a society represents an investment by that society and the able-bodied and skilled man will be capable of giving a greater return (i.e. capital-producing) than the young and old who are capital-absorbing. Expenditure on (or investment in) housing has a high capital : output ratio (i.e. a relatively low return) and where capital is scarce and population increase very great the proportion of investment in housing becomes very large. Admittedly the cost of supporting a child is less than supporting an old person and since the productive years of the child lie ahead it probably represents a better investment, but in this context it is the vast mass of children requiring support and, increasingly, education that keeps standards at subsistence level and absorbs capital so urgently needed for economic development in more remunerative sectors of the economy. In other words heavy increase of population is likely to reduce output per head unless considerable investment is possible. Economists have suggested a capital : output ratio of up to 4 to 1 may be needed to maintain living standards. This suggests that a population growth of 2 per cent will need a net investment of 8 per cent of the national income to maintain existing standards of living. Few developing lands manage to invest more than 5–6 per cent per annum of their national income and this means that unless other investment becomes available such a population increase will bring about a fall in living standards.

An important point of impact upon the economy is when at the age of about fifteen years masses of work-seeking adolescents annually swamp the labour market. A few years ago the Indian Finance Minister stated that four million new jobs had been created during the first four years of India's first Five Year Plan, but that the natural increase to the population during this period had thrust seven million new job-seekers on to the labour market. Japan also may be cited; even with industry developing at a higher pace than between the wars it is not expected that employment can be found for more than half the million who join the labour force each year. Such a number of youths competing for not enough jobs might well depress the level of wages and perpetuate the very conditions of poverty it is sought to end. Alternatively where minimum wage safeguards exist, much purchasing power may go into the pockets of those who have few commitments or responsibilities and little predisposition to save. The legalizing of abortion in 1952 contributed to a sharp reduction in births in Japan during the post-war period. However, well over a million seek to join the labour force each year. These figures give some idea of the magnitude of the scale of development now becoming necessary to keep pace with the current heavy natural increase of population. It is small wonder that all too frequently we read that economic advance in so many developing lands is being cancelled-out by the rate man is multiplying.

There are further important aspects of juvenility, one being its bearing on fecundity. The unusually large increments at the base of these population pyramids with the passing of years will expand the reproductive age groups: a young population is a highly fecund population. This favours a continuance of high birth rates unless other factors such as later marriage or greater application of birth control reduce fertility. As such factors are usually the outcome of a rising standard of living they are difficult to accomplish with such prolific population. In 1947 about 42 per cent of Japanese women were in the child-bearing age groups (15–45 years), by 1962 this proportion was 50 per cent. Such a proportional increase may not seem too serious but, in fact, it represents over six million more potential mothers.

Other aspects of juvenility not often comprehended are socio-political. In young populations the enthusiasm, impatience, intolerance and disillusionment of youth do not lack expression. The student demonstrations and riots now becoming characteristic draw much of their vigour from the sheer preponderance of the young in their communities. In Japan more than two-fifths of the population is under 20; in Sri Lanka the proportion is almost a half. It is not only in the West that the teenager has assumed such social and economic importance.

The population explosion of the recent decades and hitherto the low expectation of life in most of the developing lands indicate that their immediate problems concern youth rather than old age. The economic problems associated with ageing populations are now being met in many countries in the low fluctuating population stage and mainly stem from the growing proportion of the pensionable population which constitutes an increasing burden on the body of productive workers. Other and less tangible problems may arise from the changing mental outlook of such populations: less flexibility and go-aheadness may become perceptible. However, these situations are still relatively remote in under-developed lands where an increasing span of life should imply a healthier and more productive working force to sustain both young and old dependents.

Massive emigration is sometimes advanced as a solution to the problems of surplus populations. There is much literature discussing the efficacy and practicability of substantial movements of population, and it is sufficient here to say that history shows that emigration offers little or no relief when high birth rates persist. In theory, however, with a falling birth rate and a rising standard of living the removal of a part of the population might have an upward effect upon the economy. This ignores the general impracticability of such measures: numbers are now too vast, receiving areas inadequate and unwelcoming, the capital costs immense. Further, even with low living standards prodigious capital would be required for the provision of homes, utilities and social services compatible with a reasonable standard of living. To remove from one slum to create another would be no solution.

URBANIZATION

A further and important manifestation of increasing populations in the lesser-developed lands is in the remarkable increase of the urban portions of the population. Much has yet to be done in recording the distribution of population in these countries, but the increase in the size and number of towns has become characteristic and the rural : urban ratio of these populations is altering. The tendency for urban growth with increasing population, and particularly with growing economic development, is well established. The application of power and the introduction of factory industry saw the beginning of the ascendancy of town over countryside in the developed lands. Towns became workplaces and, as standards rose, service activities grew also: culture wants became added to creature wants. To overcrowded under-employed rural populations towns offer greater opportunity of casual employment, wages are usually better than in the countryside (although living costs are higher too) and they attract by the amenities they offer: electric light, water, health clinics, a chance of a new life. The first signs of development appear in the towns, in the utilities, services and amusement amenities: all act as magnets in attracting further population.

The degree of urbanization is yet unmeasured in many lands and, since there is no universal acceptance of the point at which a village becomes a town, it is unlikely that precise data will ever be available. However, at the upper end of the scale the number, size and growth of cities of over a million people – 'million' cities – is known with tolerable accuracy. Their numbers have increased over six-fold between 1925 and 1970, and from containing 2·9 per cent of world population they had come to hold 10 per cent. This represents a rate of growth of 'million' cities faster than that of world population. Cairo may be taken as typical. Between 1937 and 1970 its population grew by 280 per cent, nearly three times the rate for Egypt as a whole. Two further significant facts emerge: a snowball effect is discernible in that the larger or 'multi-million' cities show a faster rate of growth and that the greatest developments are in the lower latitudes. This is to be expected in that development has lagged in so many of these mainly agricultural countries and rapid urbanization is a reflection of startling population increase and the beginning of economic development. In the early 1950s some eighty 'million' cities accommodated 192·5 million people;[2] two decades later in the early 1970s, there were 151 such cities with a total population of 380 million people. Here we have taken the 'million' city as a loose index of urbanization, for each 'million' city is supported by dozens of smaller cities and towns. The rapid growth of towns in the warmer latitudes since the Second World War has been remarkable, but it is likely to prove only the beginning of such a movement and must be taken as an expression of the radical changes in economy and way of life now being engendered.

In addition to the many economic benefits accruing from urbanization which will be discussed later, there are distinct social advantages. Agglomeration of population allows the provision of utilities such as water and power supplies, transport services, education and health provision (hospitals and clinics). In the developing lands where urban occupations are expanding and agricultural ones are relatively declining real income per head is generally higher in urban employment and it is in the towns that a rise of living standards first becomes apparent. The spread of education, the desire for comforts and amenities, the raising of the status of women, the growing means of enjoying leisure hours all begin to shape a new mode of life in which children play a less prominent part. Further, with the eventual introduction of compulsory full-time education and establishment of minimum ages of employment, children cease to be an economic asset but instead may represent an encumbrance to social and material advancement. These conditions underlie the well-known fact that urban birth rates are generally lower than rural ones. 'The more urban an area the lower the fertility of the population and the more rural an area the more rapidly its population is reproducing' (T. Lynn Smith). This is precisely a state of affairs urgently to be attained in the world's developing lands. The evolution of a social milieu where the small family is the rule first in the town and then in the country is urgently needed but is yet a long way off.

QUALITY OF POPULATION

In Chapter 1 reference was made to the importance of population 'quality', a term used here to indicate in the broadest sense the physical and mental conditions of a people: their degree of health, education, skill, adaptability, liveliness. These attitudes of a society bear some relation to environmental and demographic conditions and while less tangible than capital or raw material resources nevertheless may prove decisive in particular development situations. In this sense the poor 'quality' of their population is probably the greatest handicap to the economic advance of the developing lands. Most of their populations, particularly in the tropical areas, are disease-ridden and undernourished and constitute a great drag on development. A circular pattern can be identified: ill-health = reduced working capacity = lower productivity = poverty = under-nourishment = ill-health.

Nutritional diseases such as pellagra, beri-beri and rickets are prevalent. In themselves they are not heavily fatal but they so debilitate and sap the resistance that endemic and infectious diseases such as cholera, typhus and malaria take immense toll. Not only are diets inadequate in amount (under-nutrition), but they are usually ill-balanced (malnutrition), with serious protein and fat deficiencies and over-emphasis on starch. In Egypt the average daily intake of calories per person in 1952 was 2340 (this implies many thousands had less than this amount) whereas dieticians have estimated that the minimum level for well-being in Egypt is 2400 calories. The mass of peasantry eats very little meat, fish, milk or eggs but subsists mainly on cereals (principally maize). In Cairo in 1939 45 per cent of children under 2 years of age and 80 per cent under 10 years showed signs of rickets. Kwashiorkor or protein malnutrition of young children is another product of these conditions where the period of lactation is reduced and weaning is upon starchy diets such as banana, maize and tapioca. Many of these children die and of those who survive the prevalence of cancer of the liver in later life has been noticed. A survey in Perak, Malaya, in 1959 showed that out of a random selection of 200 children eighty-eight showed some signs of protein deficiency and thirty-eight had kwashiorkor. One toddler's diet mentioned in the survey consisted of sweetened black coffee, soft rice and water for the main meal and rice and water again in the evening if the child desired it.

These nutritional diseases debilitate and allow a wider incidence of diseases such as malaria, estimated to affect some 300 million people in the world each year. Gourou has pointed out that the most serious fact about malaria is that each death it causes corresponds to at least 2000 days of illness.[3] Much of the apathy of the Egyptian fellahin and tolerance towards their wretched conditions of life has been ascribed to the vicious hold of the intestinal worm diseases bilharzia and ankylostoma – at one time affecting three-quarters of the rural population. These diseases are caught from parasites carried by snails in the irrigation waters. They rarely cause death but sap the vitality, dull the mind, engender feelings of apathy and resignation and reduce the capacity and output of Egyptian labour.

It is difficult for people living in temperate latitudes to appreciate the real significance of disease as a factor retarding the development of a tropical area. The native of West Africa inherits almost all the disorders of temperate climates, and on top of these he may suffer from a multitude of other diseases to which his ignorance of their causes, his poor standards of hygiene and his particular environment make him liable. The inadequacy of the medical facilities and often the reluctance of the sufferers to take advantage of them at least until it is too late aggravates the situation. Trypanosomiasis and onchocerciasis . . . epidemics of cerebrospinal meningitis, the major outbreaks of which have affected the whole of the savana belt of West Africa for at least the past fifty years, occur frequently. Smallpox, malaria, bilharzia, yaws and intestinal disorders are endemic.[4]

Great advances are being made in the eradication of these conditions thanks to the greater use of the new antibiotic drugs such as DDT and penicillin and improvements in hygiene and sanitation. In one sense the cost has been small in comparison with the immediate benefits. The northern province of Thailand, for example, was cleansed of malaria at a cost of 5p per head of its population. The benefits are widespread: mortality has decreased and there is greater productivity from both man and beast, freed not merely from malaria but also from fly-borne dysentery, typhoid and ticks. These advances, however, also have a debit side, for unless the resultant death control becomes matched by birth control, or the means of greater productivity are available, then malnourishment and malnutrition may increase. The situation in part of eastern Bangladesh exemplifies this. In the last few years eradication of malaria has led to 15 per cent greater productivity from the rice fields, but fewer of the healthier workers are needed and rural unemployment has increased, for no fresh land is available to put under cultivation. There is no doubt that, in general, productivity per worker in the under-developed lands is low but with betterment of health it can be considerably improved. This in turn presents further economic and social problems.

Illiteracy is another serious drawback to the advancement of these populations and is the result of the quite inadequate provisions for, and scope of, elementary education in most of these lands. To millions the world is little more than the village and its contiguous fields, where the methods and sequences of the agrarian life, hallowed by tradition, take their predestined course year after year. It is this illiteracy and general ignorance, coupled with the ingrained resistance to change, that is proving a formidable obstacle in furthering hygiene, in disseminating birth-control information, in introducing new crops or methods of husbandry, in advancing manufacturing industry. Many of these countries have in the past spent much money upon university education for the favoured few: the broad bases of the educational pyramids have been neglected. The task of raising the abysmally low level of popular education in the developing lands of the world is gigantic and will take decades to accomplish, but it has begun. Illiteracy in Egypt in the thirty years from 1940 declined from 75 to 55 per cent of the population, but in India the rate has only dropped from 85 to 72 per cent.

To provide and develop successfully a substantial industrial segment in the economies of the developing lands will require a considerable raising of the quality of their populations. The conversion of illiterate, undernourished, apathetic and disease-ridden agricultural workers into alert, healthy and skilled industrial operatives will prove a costly, lengthy and difficult metamorphosis. Even more important will be the emergence of the smaller number of men prepared to take risks in investment and innovation, no longer putting their money into land but bringing in science, new techniques and adventuring into industry. Governmental action may supplement or surpass their efforts but the need for these entrepreneurs is vital. In short, the whole outlook of such societies must undergo reorientation. Education is the key that must open eyes to possibilities and society should become permeated with the idea of development, perhaps even dedicated to it as in China and USSR where government and people alike are intent on making up for lost years in the shortest possible time. In all this one condition would seem to be paramount, namely the reduction of the birth rates of these populations. Without fewer births the work of medicine and science will be jeopardized: numbers increasing at an ever-faster rate may depress levels of nutrition even more, increasing under-employment spread apathy and misery, while the provision of education for the growing mass of children may become more and more beyond the resources of the countries concerned.

BIBLIOGRAPHICAL REFERENCES

1. P. T. Bauer and B. S. Yamey, *The Economics of Under-developed Countries* (Cambridge, 1959), p. 31, and W. A. Lewis, *The Theory of Economic Growth* (London, 1955), pp. 201–13.
2. D. L. Linton, 'Millionaire Cities Today and Yesterday', *Geography* (1958), p. 253, and A. B. Mountjoy, 'Million Cities: Urbanisation and the Developing Countries', *Geography* (1968), pp. 365–374.
3. P. Gourou, *The Tropical World* (London, 1961), p. 7.
4. T. E. Hilton, 'Land Planning and Resettlement in Northern Ghana', *Geography* (1959), p. 230.

J. Beaujeu-Garnier, *Geography of Population* (London, 1966).
F. Osborn (Ed.), *Our Crowded Planet* (London, 1963).
J. I. Clarke, *Population Geography and the Developing Countries* (Oxford, 1971).
G. T. Trewartha, *The Less-developed Realm: A Geography of its Population* (London, 1972).
United Nations, *Demographic Yearbooks* (annually).

4 Industrialization – the panacea?

In the preceding chapters the value and advantages to be derived from industrialization have been implied. It is appropriate now to consider more precisely the reasons why under-developed lands, many with apparently the most primitive economies, desire so earnestly to further manufacturing industry. It is clear that a whole range of reasons may be cited, dependent upon the individual circumstances of the countries, but broadly we may cite three conditions that such lands wish to ameliorate, and go on to consider just why the development of manufacturing industry is regarded as the best means of such amelioration. The three customary objects of industrialization policies are to provide work for growing populations (and in some cases for already under-employed agricultural populations), to raise the standard of living by increasing the per capita net national income and, often, to improve balance of payment situations. Various other reasons have sometimes been cited or imputed in particular cases, one especially being the desire for national prestige which an industrial economy could give over fellow primary producers. Yugoslavia, Argentina and Egypt have been mentioned in such a context and East Germany under her first two Five Year Plans. There is indeed a connection between the political revolution and the social and economic ones they heralded; by many it is held that the one is the essential precursor of the other. The danger of industrialization being pursued purely for nationalistic ends is that such policies may lead to autarky and a development programme based upon uneconomic desires for industrial self-sufficiency, rather than a furthering of primary production where comparative advantage is held over competitors and the development of those industries most likely to have good economic bases.

The most noticeable effect of development which the under-developed lands can see in the wealthy lands is the mass of manufacturing industry from which the wealth, power and poise of the developed world appears to emanate. Consequently it is not surprising that the introduction of manufacturing industry should be regarded uncritically as a panacea by many members of the have-not nations. Fortunately, major industrial and development schemes nowadays nearly all come under the close scrutiny of international experts, particularly if international capital is sought for them, and this acts as a check on wilder promotions that might have little prospect of success. It should be made clear that the switching of a large mass of humanity to industrial pursuits is in itself no answer to the world's population problem. We have still not reached the state when we can cheaply mass-produce synthetic food from inanimate matter in our factories, and new industrial populations still need to be fed. It is, of course, in the prospect of greater returns accruing from manufacturing industry making possible the purchase of food from food-surplus countries, as is done in much of northwest Europe, that the hopes of the poorer lands lie. It must be noticed, however, that this state of affairs does not occur overnight, and initially indigenous supplies of food need to be increased, if at all possible, to feed the growing urban-industrial population and thus preserve capital for re-investment rather than spend it on imported foodstuffs. It follows that developments in agriculture must not be neglected and should continue with industrial development, a situation frequently to be mentioned in the following chapters, although our prime concern is with industry.

OCCUPATIONAL STRUCTURES

As we have seen, it is possible to classify the cycle of population development into stages; in turn it is thought that the cycle of economic development is susceptible to a similar analysis and that stages of economic development may be discovered and classified. Foremost in this field is the work of W. W. Rostow, in whose view an economy moves from a traditional stage through a take-off period to sustained growth, maturity and a stage of high mass-consumption.[1] Development implies changing emphases within an economy, and this is evidenced in the shifting distribution of labour among the major kinds of activity. Colin Clark in his book *The Conditions of Economic Progress* makes a now widely accepted simple division of production into primary, secondary and tertiary groups. The primary activities include farming, fishing and forestry; secondary production includes mining, manufacturing and public utilities such as gas and electricity production; and tertiary production includes all other activities, such as transport, distribution, public administration, entertainment, etc.[2]

From the beginning of time primary activities have been basic to man's existence, and development signifies a movement whereby primary activities continue, but with increasing efficiency so that labour is released for other work involving more application of science, invention and capital. Thus we shall expect the under-developed countries to have an overwhelming proportion of their working population engaged in agriculture with quite small proportions in secondary and tertiary occupations, while fully developed lands might show an opposite pattern. In fact, under-developed lands have around 60–70 per cent of their labour force engaged in primary production, whereas developed countries that have entered the stage of maturity generally have less than 20 per cent thus engaged.

Throughout the world agricultural incomes per head tend to be less than non-agricultural incomes. Sometimes, as in Australia, the differences are not great but, for example, in Indonesia non-agricultural income per head is five times higher than agricultural income. Such a discrepancy is a measure of under-development and, given the opportunity, spurs labour away to other sectors of the economy. A developed economy gives a high per capita income since it is associated with a more varied economic structure whereby science and capital play an increasing part, and agriculture, using a smaller proportion of the labour force, functions with higher efficiency.

These features are demonstrated in Table 4, where it will be seen that in the case of Britain only 4 per cent of our working population is engaged in primary activities, the lowest proportion for any country, whereas nearly half are engaged in secondary activities, one of the highest for any country. The special character of our mercantile economy is reflected here, but it should be remembered that the small agricultural labour force produces nearly half the food these crowded islands need. Agricultural efficiency is steadily improving; an increase of capital invested allows each farm-worker to cultivate an increasing number of acres while a greater application of science raises productivity per acre. In 1957 one British farm-worker produced enough food for twenty people, the Australian farm-worker enough for thirty-two people, and the New Zealander for sixty-two people. The development of the United States may be interpreted from her changing occupational structure. The proportions for 1969 are quoted in Table 4, but in 1870 the three groups of activity

Table 4: *Occupational structures of selected countries, 1967–9* *

Country	Per cent of total active labour force		
	Primary activities	Secondary activities	Tertiary activities
United Kingdom	4	47	49
Belgium	6	45	49
France	16	40	44
Western Germany	10	49	41
Sweden	10	40	50
Switzerland	11	51	38
Italy	21	42	37
USSR	30	32	38
USA	9	38	53
Brazil	58	17	25
Egypt	51	14	35
Algeria	72	12	16
Japan	20	41	39
India	69	11	20
Philippines	56	15	29
Australia	10	46	44
New Zealand	13	39	48

*The figures refer to the latest year available.
SOURCES: *Yearbook of Labour Statistics*, International Labour Office, Geneva (various years).

claimed respectively 53 per cent, 23 per cent, and 24 per cent of the labour force. During the century the numbers of workers in the agricultural sector fell from a maximum of 11·6 to 4·5 million, but the volume of agricultural production increased two and three-quarter times.

From a comparison of the more advanced and less advanced countries in the table it may be deduced that as the primary (mainly agricultural) proportions of the working population declines that engaged in secondary (manufacturing) production increases: a further indicator of economic growth. The demand for foodstuffs is relatively inelastic and as real incomes rise a lesser proportion of the increase is spent on food, thus stimulating the demand for manufactured goods and services. The reasons for the growing proportions engaged in tertiary activities are not always fully understood nor the reasons why, in the eyes of some, the higher the proportion thus engaged the further the stage of economic development. Tertiary activities include a wide range of occupations, some such as 'pop-singers' and 'beauticians' virtually unproductive in the strict economic sense and others such as dockers and lorry drivers clearly vital to a modern economy. The most numerous members of this group are in shopkeeping, domestic service, sport and entertainment. To claim that the greater proportion of these strange bedfellows in an economy the more developed it is may seem odd, but it should be remembered that also in this group are clerks, accountants, directors, bankers, under-writers, teachers, inventors and the professional classes who, by and large, smooth, direct and control the economy.

THE DISABILITIES OF AGRICULTURE

The fact that throughout the world agriculture is reaching or entering the stage of decreasing returns whereas industry, in the main, goes on under conditions of increasing returns raises the question of the differences between the two activities, and in particular the disadvantages of agriculture *vis-à-vis* manufacturing industry. The fundamental disadvantage under which agriculture labours is that the farmer has virtually no control over the natural forces of the physical environment which he utilizes. His crops depend upon sunshine, water, air and mineral salts and while locally farmers may irrigate or drain, add fertilizer or trace elements to their soils, by and large it is the environment that calls the tune. From this stem a number of other disadvantages, not least being that yields vary from year to year according to the ravages of weather, disease and pests. Consequently farmers cannot foretell accurately the volume of their production each year. Further, production is generally slower than in manufacturing industry, requiring farmers to look ahead and estimate the character of the market at least a year in advance. Crops and animals take months to mature and slow down farmers' reactions to changes in demand, for once crops are in the ground and animals fattening most farmers prefer to reap their crops, shear their sheep, pick their cocoa beans and so on despite glut conditions and falling prices. These factors all help to account for the considerable price fluctuations, alternating with gluts and shortages, notable in primary production and of serious consequences to steady economic progress in developing lands. The seasonal character of farming operations in many parts of the world may well impose uneconomic use of labour and certainly of machinery. Farming machinery is costly and is generally of a specialized character and may only be in use for a few weeks each year, a great contrast to most factory machinery which may be in almost continual operation.

For the relative inflexibility of agriculture there are a number of reasons, not all of them economic. In many parts of the world the traditional conservatism of the peasantry may present a formidable bulwark to progress, especially where the agricultural way of life has become intimately interwoven into the fabric of society, and where changes in agriculture might presage deep repercussions on social groupings and ways of life. This is exemplified in many parts of Africa where the white man's concept of the individual ownership of land has conflicted severely with the natives' concept of tribal ownership and use. Similarly the threat of far-reaching changes in their way of life reinforced peasant opposition to the USSR and East European attempts at collectivization. Agriculture is also at some disadvantage when there is a preponderance of agrarian population, for the onset of decreasing returns comes more swiftly than with industry. Much of the poverty in many developing lands is attributable to this: pressure of population with no alternative employment forcing far too many into agriculture. Labour is applied beyond the point of decreasing returns with consequent inefficiency and low productivity per head.

A further serious drawback lies in the relative inelasticity of demand for agricultural products. The bulk of the products of agriculture are foodstuffs and, being vital to life, are already consumed in great quantities; consequently relatively little extra food is bought if prices fall. Equally, if incomes rise, a less than proportionate extra amount is spent on food: instead, the sale of manufactured goods is stimulated. This suggests that as the developed lands have become richer the primary producers selling them their agricultural produce have received a less than proportionate share in the increased wealth. From this it would seem that international trade in primary products does not really produce the equalizing tendencies often claimed for it, but tends to work in favour of the industrialized nations. Even the fruits of greater efficiency of production may not be passed on to the primary producers. Surplus rural populations offering a mass of unskilled labour at the lowest of wages all too often act as a disincentive to greater efficiency and resist innovation. However, where improvements take place, and exports are produced more cheaply, the inelasticity of demand prevents the enlargement of the market, which might bring the response of greater productivity and employment, instead the advantages of the cheaper production accrue to the importing country.

A further factor telling against the exporters of primary produce is the greater effect of technical progress upon industry than upon agriculture. This contributes to the fact that industrial countries succeed in increasing their output without a proportionate increase in their imports of raw materials. This comes about in various ways: greater efficiency and reduction of waste; relative decline in textiles which have a high raw material content; the increasing use of synthetic substitutes, such as plastics, man-made fibres, synthetic rubber and dyestuffs. It must be appreciated that the development of synthetics and substitutes is related to price and cost factors. To some extent the general failure of the developing countries to reduce costs and prices of their primary exports relative to those of the developed countries has spurred on invention and technological progress. It has been estimated that in the major industrial countries synthetic materials now account for about 15 per cent of the raw materials used in manufacture whereas the proportion was barely 3 per cent before the Second World War. But for this, imports of natural raw material into these major industrial countries might be 40 per cent higher than they are at present. In all, for every £100 worth of manufactures produced the total import of fuel and raw material declined from £26 in 1938 to £21 in 1955. The weight of these disabilities set against the corresponding advantages lying with manufacturing industry help to account for the situation where the primary producers were left behind in the development race. The decade of the 1950s saw the terms of trade swing adversely against the developing countries' primary exports, for whereas export prices of manufactured goods rose by 20 per cent, export prices of primary products rose by only 5 per cent. During the 1960s raw material and fuel export prices declined slightly, but prices of foodstuffs exports rose; however, a 40 per cent increase in the cost of manufactured goods continued the adverse terms of trade pattern. It was not until the early 1970s, when widespread growth in developed economies was unmatched by adequate expansion of primary products and saw shortages and heavy price rises, that terms of trade began to swing in favour of the developing countries. Thus the experience of the last quarter century is that the primary producers' share in the expanding world economy is generally far less than that of the industrialized countries.

THE RELATIVE ADVANTAGES OF MANUFACTURING INDUSTRY

On the other side of the coin, the advantages that manufacturing industry holds over primary production might be considered as distinct from the disadvantages of primary production. First it must be recognized that manufacturing industry is far more flexible in methods, competition and output than agriculture. While decreasing returns may be expected in industry as in agriculture they are, in fact, usually postponed by continual improvements in techniques, by the frequent introduction of new inventions and improved machinery (far less typical in agriculture) and by increasing specialization and division of labour raising the efficiency and productivity of the labour force. The character and scale of operation are also more favourable: it is possible to control production much more closely than with farming, and supply – of a standard quality – can be trimmed more closely to demand, making for greater price stability.

It will be realized that the farmer may have to brief his labour force daily, their tasks depending on the weather, but in a factory it is possible to manage a far larger labour force because their activities are specialized and regular and generally entirely insulated from vagaries of weather. Consequently advantages of scale lie with manufacturing industry which by its organization and specialism aims at mass production through increasing efficiency and the application of power. It is, of course, basically through the application of inanimate energy that manufacturing industry offers greater productivity per worker than agriculture and the amount of power available to each worker is sometimes taken as an indicator of economic stature (Table 8).

Another advantage to industry but disadvantage to the farmer lies in the proportion of operating costs to fixed costs. A very high proportion of farm costs are in fixed charges and, relatively, the cost of seed, labour, etc., is small. This is a further factor in explaining the sluggish response to adverse conditions, for contraction of a farmer's output in times of difficulty saves relatively less than contraction of a factory's output. In the factory a far higher proportion of costs is in raw materials, labour and services, and these can be more readily cut down. It is the operation and interplay of such factors that help to account for the present state of affairs where so much of world agriculture operates under decreasing returns, whereas manufacturing industry yet shows increasing returns.

C

EFFECTS OF AGRARIAN OVER-POPULATION

In most development the two major goals are the provision of work for growing populations, and the raising of standards of living. The degree to which these aims may be realized seems to depend primarily on the demographic situation in each country. Countries with population problems are faced with the double task, those without such a problem have a much more straightforward path to raising standards of living. It is, of course, possible to envisage populations (e.g. in the British West Indies) too heavy for their agricultural resources but insufficient to sustain large-scale industrial development. As has been discussed, capacity to support population depends upon the character of the economy: an industrial economy can carry a higher population before the onset of diminishing returns than an agricultural one. If population increases over the years and the economy stagnates – possibly as a result of restricted ownership of land or social conditions where equal division of property between the heirs (as in some Moslem countries) leads to a state of chronic and uneconomic fragmentation – then a situation may well be reached when a country's agricultural output will not increase with a further increase of agricultural population. This state of affairs indicates an extreme form of over-population, a stage beyond that occurring with the onset of diminishing returns (where increase of population brings a less than proportionate increase of production). Not many countries have reached the extreme state, although a number are generally considered to be on the brink, among them Java, Egypt and Barbados.

Over-population, then, should always be thought of as relative to a country's economy. As we have seen, not all under-developed agricultural lands are over-populated although many in Asia are, to which may be added Egypt, and the British West Indies. In many under-developed lands the poverty of the masses may be related sometimes to land tenure systems whereby there is an institutional monopoly of land and therefore of capital (as in many states of Latin America), sometimes to poor farming reinforced by social and religious taboos exhausting the soil (as in India), sometimes to naturally poor soils, leached or waterlogged, where the application of considerable capital for irrigation or drainage is necessary in order to raise yields. There is, in fact a wide range of immediate causes of poverty and under-development. It is in the heavily populated under-developed lands that prevailing conditions constitute the greatest spur to development since they build up to increasing unrest, or even anarchy or revolution.

It must not be thought that in over-populated agrarian countries there are necessarily vast masses of unemployed. The onset of over-population is slow and insidious and demonstrates itself rather by growing poverty and increasing under-employment. Excessive numbers are to be found in domestic service, casual employment, and agriculture; one notices a proliferation of newsvendors, boot-blacks, porters and petty traders – all doing little business and earning barely enough for subsistence. Similarly in agriculture more and more labour finds employment on the land until the marginal productivity of labour is zero, or even negative. This situation may well lead to a loss of soil fertility by the reduction of fallow periods, lack of manuring and over-cropping. This results in falling output per acre and not merely falling output per head. The term 'disguised unemployment' is sometimes used to describe an element of the working population that can be regarded as surplus in the sense that if it was removed from the land the volume of production would not fall. It is in this context that the massive population of South-east Asia, with 70–80 per cent of the workers toiling on the land, should be viewed.

The results of increasing population pressure, slowly grinding poverty, are similar everywhere. The process of descent to such an abject situation may take different forms, generally related to the system of land tenure. These systems are numerous in their variations but may be reduced essentially to three major types:

1. Communal ownership, usually tribal as in much of Africa (e.g. Basutoland, parts of Zambia and Zaïre) where there is considerable scope for agricultural improvement to raise living standards;

2. Peasant proprietorship, demonstrated in other parts of Africa such as Ghana and Uganda, but where the middle-man and village usurer may play a significant role and where holdings become reduced below economic size and owners must offer their labour to larger farmers in order to support their families;

3. Large estate farming, of which we may distinguish three types – latifundia, zamindari and plantation. Latifundia are characteristic of southern Europe and Latin America where the larger part of the estate is farmed extensively with hired labour, while the lesser part may be let on a share-cropping basis. In the zamindari system, more

prevalent in Asia, the estate is let out in small holdings to tenant farmers on a money rent or share-cropping basis. Plantation estates are usually owned by foreign capital and operated by foreign management, and are efficient large-scale enterprises employing hired labour.

It is instructive to observe the changes, both social and economic, that evolve as pressure of workers on the land increases. The large estates being farmed under the latifundian and plantation systems have a relatively inelastic demand for labour and the more seeking work, the more the level of wages tends to be depressed. Equally, where land is let for rent the increasing numbers desiring land force up rents and land prices to crippling levels. Share-cropping tenancies also become subjected to increasingly unfavourable terms. By 1960 the share of revenue paid to landowners in rents in Oriental countries had come to be out of all proportion to the total productivity of agriculture and to the services the landlord offered. Rent (in various combinations of cash, produce and labour) claimed between one-third and one-half of the gross output value of agriculture in Middle East and South-east Asian countries.[3] Where conditions of increasing population and limited farmland persist many of the great land-owners are absentees. A combination of absentee landlords, high rents, short leases and impoverished peasantry may eventually lead to ruin of the land for there is neither the incentive nor the wherewithal to improve fertility, but the greatest encouragement to get as much as possible from the soil.

The demographic element has further important effects of both geographical and economic significance. As population pressure mounts so do farming character and technique respond. As more and more labour becomes applied, so more labour-intensive methods become adopted (e.g. removing spade-excavated earth from new canals in Egypt by baskets on camels and in India by human porterage) and more labour-intensive crops become grown. Quality and variety of crops are sacrificed to quantity : where subsistence farming predominates the most labour-demanding and highest food-yielding plants oust all others and virtual monoculture appears, as in the case of rice in the delta lands of South-east Asia. On large properties where commercial crops are grown cotton becomes favoured as one of the most labour-intensive of the industrial crops, it is also liked by absentee 'gentlemen farmers' because an impoverished peasantry cannot eat it. In short, it is true to say that farming and tenure systems mould themselves to growing populations, absorbing more and more labour but under increasingly unfavourable conditions as the law of diminishing returns comes into play.

This chain of human misery is incomplete without recognition of the additional and concomitant social consequences. Under such conditions the power and wealth of the landowning classes expand while the mass of the peasantry grows poorer, creating in these agrarian societies a deep gulf between the governing class and the bulk of the population, for a middle or professional and commercial class is too small to span the gap. Money becomes concentrated into the hands of a very few while the mass of the population lives at a level of poverty not readily comprehended in the West. This means that there is virtually no saving and thus a very low rate of capital accumulation and reinvestment. To the wealthy, land is the principal source of wealth and has first claim on further investment, otherwise much tends to be spent on ostentatious living.

We now see that a root cause of the abysmal conditions of the mass of the peasantry in many lands is the excess of hands at work and mouths to be fed – the 'surplus' element in the agrarian population which also provides a disincentive to agricultural improvement. This situation is characteristic of many countries extending from South-eastern Europe through South-east Asia to China and is also found in the Caribbean area. It is not common in Africa and South America but is probably beginning in parts of Central America. Obviously it is not possible to estimate closely the proportion of the surplus element in these populations. Estimates in the 1930s for some South-east European countries were as high as 25–30 per cent of the agricultural labour force, the proportion in Egypt is probably rather higher, while for India an estimate of at least a quarter has been made (representing 30–40 million people).[4] By their presence these millions drag down the general level of living and, in the sense that if their labour were removed the volume of production would not suffer, they contribute nothing to productivity. The magnitude of the problem is becoming greatly increased with the impact of the medical revolution leading to improvements in the health of the peasantry.

As these conditions move from bad to worse unrest frequently increases. Landowners tend to become more obstinate and reactionary in their resistance to change. Reforms often wait upon crisis and even anarchy (southern Italy, 1950); upon political revolution (Mexico, Egypt); or follow the upheavals of war (Bulgaria, 1880;

Yugoslavia, 1918 and 1945). The redistribution of land at the expense of the great landlords is an early reform and under certain conditions can have a number of beneficial effects (see p. 178). However, the main problem of too many people on too little land remains, no matter how the ownership is juggled with, and acts as the most powerful incentive to an introduction or expansion of an industrial sector in the economy.

Thus the most weighty factor in the movement for development lies in the abysmal and worsening conditions that can occur under a combination of primary production, population pressure and maldistributed land ownership and tenure. The theory of greater returns and higher living standards from manufacturing industry is easy to grasp and in practice even where industry is only in its infancy begins to make itself felt. For example, whereas the annual income of the Egyptian fellah was estimated at £E8 in 1944 the annual income of the Egyptian industrial worker was around £E50, while in Uganda in 1968 the income per head in industry was estimated at over twice the income per head in agriculture. These comparisons may not be pressed too far, for it is not easy to be precise in valuing the self-sufficient element of the farmer, while industrial workers generally live under urban conditions where living costs are much higher.

THE SOCIAL AND DEMOGRAPHIC EFFECTS OF
INDUSTRIALIZATION

Particularly in its early stage, manufacturing industry is related to the urban centres where market, labour and a range of public utilities are available. Some writers suggest that the ideal industrial development in developing countries should be one of dispersal among rural areas where so much surplus labour is available. This is very much an idealized solution and for many reasons is not practicable, especially in early stages. Furthermore, such developments are less likely to capitalize a range of social opportunities and advantages that the development of urban communities makes possible. The agglomeration of people makes it easier and cheaper to provide social, educational, police, sanitary and health facilities, as well as to install such services as piped water, main drainage, gas and electricity. A far higher scale of creature comforts becomes possible and attainable than in the village. Imported goods in the shops give glimpses and knowledge both of a wider world and a high standard of attainment, and desires are raised that become the spur to better-

⸱nt. Education and training are seen as the keys to better living
⸱⸱se are more readily available in the towns. However, in the
⸱t is of transcendent importance that with education and
⸱ndards of living the size of family will be reduced by
⸱tes, as has happened in the West.
⸱⸱⸱⸱⸱⸱⸱⸱ ⸱en stressed that the only real and ultimate solution
to the world's population problem is a reduction of birth rates
broadly commensurate with the fast-dropping death rate. Development to be completely successful should not only raise living standards and give more employment but should create conditions that
eventually bring birth rates down; industrialization alone will not
solve the economic problems of such countries as India, Java, China
and Egypt. Despite much study the mechanism by which this has
happened in the developed countries of Europe and their overseas
offshoots can only be postulated in rather general terms. It is certain
that industrialization in itself does not explain the reduction in the
size of families, for whereas Britain certainly was industrialized the
overseas Dominions were still heavily agricultural when their birth
rates began to fall; moreover in their cases neither could the spur of
population pressure be cited. Carr-Saunders has pointed out that these
countries and Western Europe (and rather later Eastern and Southern
Europe) shared a similar mode of life, food, clothes, social fashions
and conventions. The practice of family limitation spread among
these closely associated countries much as any new habits and novel
ideas spread.[5] In other words, attitudes gradually changed as a result
of changing social and economic conditions, and not, for example,
through any sudden new knowledge of birth-control methods.

Development, embracing urbanization and education, takes a
large share in the establishment of the conditions for such changing
of social conventions and attitudes. Pure water supplies, improved
sanitation and medical facilities in towns reduce the toll on young
children and make it unnecessary for eight children to be born in
order to rear four. Parents come to realize that the smaller the family
the greater the opportunities they can offer their children and the
easier their own passage up the social ladder. Much of this social
evolution is closely bound up with the position of women. Towns
offer women far more opportunities of education and emancipation
than the village, and with a lifetime no longer devoted to producing
and rearing numerous children employment outside the home becomes possible. All this takes time: two and possibly three generations in the developed lands. Whether the pattern will be both

followed and speeded in the present developing lands are crucial questions. In that it represents social development fructifying from economic development we might regard it as logical and inevitable. Whether a speeding up is possible remains doubtful, for these tendencies evolve, they cannot be imposed. Religious and governmental sanction might do much to clear the path, as also the spread of education and the emergence of a middle class from a newly created or enlarged proletariat; the development of social and cultural standards cannot be accomplished overnight.

It is clear that a wide range of social and economic factors and emotions are involved in accounting for the fall in birth rate that seems to be an early attendant upon a developing urban way of life. One feature deserving of mention is that for a time in developing countries urban birth rates may appear higher than rural rates, but investigation shows that this is usually due to more complete registration. In rural areas the births of a substantial number of babies may never be registered. The more difficult question, to which it would not seem possible to give a definite answer is whether, in fact, economic and social developments in the developing lands will elicit a similar demographic response to that during the past century in the Western world. It would be wrong to assume automatically that the same values will be set upon social position, upon the use of leisure and upon women's emancipation. To our eyes many of the taboos (religious and social) of a number of Asian societies seem odd and anachronistic. In a similar manner it is possible that the response to development by these people may not follow the lines of the Western logic which regards development mainly in economic terms: the move towards an industrial society, to Rostow's phase of mass consumption and to materialism.

In this context attention must be paid to the post-war demographic situation in some of the wealthiest of the developed lands, all in the fourth (low fluctuating) stage of the population cycle. We find that the high immediate post-war birth rates have been maintained (Table 5). This is surprising and we may well consider whether the thesis of industrialization and urbanization damping down birth rates is really valid after all, although allowance must be made for net immigration into the USA, Canada, Australia and New Zealand of people mainly young. It may yet be early to advance explanations, but one suspects that the population wheel is turning full circle in these countries. All of them have for some time been in the high mass-consumption stage of economic growth. Their populations

Table 5: *Rates of births, deaths and natural increase for selected countries, 1966–70**

	Crude birth rate %oo	Crude death rate %oo	Natural increase %
United Kingdom	16·2	11·6	0·5
United States	17·3	9·3	0·8
Canada	17·0	7·3	1·0
Australia	21·7	8·7	1·3
New Zealand	22·2	8·8	1·3
Costa Rica	45·1	7·6	3·8
Guatemala	39·0	15·0	2·4
Honduras	49·0	17·1	3·2
Brazil	37·8	9·5	2·8
Chile	26·6	9·0	1·6
Colombia	44·6	10·6	3·4
Guyana	38·1	6·8	3·1
Sri Lanka	29·4	7·5	2·2
India	42·8	16·7	2·6
Iraq	49·3	15·5	3·4
Japan	19·2	6·6	1·3
Sarawak	48·0	12·5	3·6
Ghana	46·6	17·8	2·9
Kenya	47·8	17·5	3·0
Morocco	49·5	16·5	3·3
Zambia	49·8	20·7	2·9

*The figures refer to the latest year available.
SOURCE: *UN Demographic Yearbook, 1972.* New York, 1973.

have previously experienced the slowing down of growth as towns grew and their economies developed, but they are now enjoying the fruits of development: their living standards are higher than ever before and the mother's and housewife's tasks eased by mechanical aids, so that having a family need no longer mean drudgery and the complete sacrifice of leisure. To this change in the material situation may be added a changing attitude of mind. The day of one and two children per family is passing: it is becoming fashionable to have more children. Other supporting arguments may be advanced; it is enough here to suggest that with growing prosperity in the developed lands their level of births in the fourth stage of the population cycle has become distinctly higher than when the stage was first entered.

It is not always appreciated that attempts to foster and expand manufacturing industry must be paralleled by development and expansion of the agricultural sector of the economy. There is no simple choice between developing either industry or agriculture, the two sectors are intimately related. Put at its simplest, the farmer should produce more in order to feed the growing population engaged in secondary and tertiary activities and he should be able to do this with a reducing labour force, for successful industrial development necessarily attracts labour from agriculture. This has been the pattern of development in Western countries and it is worth noting that the world's most efficient and productive farming is to be found in those countries, whether the criterion be output per acre or per man employed. However, in that the kind of farming tends to be wasteful of land (considerable emphasis on meat and milk and therefore 'two-stage' agriculture)[6] the supporting power or carrying capacity per acre is exceeded by certain countries such as Japan and Egypt, with their double and treble cropping and emphasis upon 'one-stage' cereal crops.

If agriculture fails to provide food for growing industrial and urban populations then much-needed capital will have to be spent on importing foodstuffs and development will be retarded. Conversely if agriculture can increase its production for export of primary raw materials, then more foreign exchange is available to aid development of the whole economy. It is of course easy to make such suggestions but for a host of varied reasons (land tenure systems, surplus agricultural population, institutional monopoly of capital) far more difficult for them to be carried out. However, a more prosperous agricultural sector is also needed to provide a market for the products of the new industries. At the moment the poverty of agriculturists and therefore the smallness of the available market for manufactured goods is probably the greatest hindrance to development. Any enlargement of purchasing power of the peasantry should act as a stimulus to industrial development – one factor cited in favour of land reform.

Hence the successful launching of programmes of industrialization depend upon improvements in agriculture, and the degree to which the improvements can be attained can either provide a curb or act as an incentive to the success of the new ventures. From this it follows that systematic improvement (and therefore investment) in agriculture must be a foremost task of the under-developed lands. The aim should be mutual self-support between these two sectors of the economy whereby agriculture's surplus population may be siphoned off into industry as agriculture, under the stimulus of greater demand becomes more efficient and industry in turn raises the market for agricultural produce. This theory underlies planned development in Communist countries and is the basis of the Commonwealth's Colombo Plan. Agriculture is one of the major existing sources of wealth in developing lands; from it they must expect to obtain a substantial proportion of the capital needed for development. Thus profits from both the ownership and the working of land need to be made available for productive investment, not only to establish new industries but particularly to sustain and nourish them during the lengthy period when they are struggling to gather momentum.

BIBLIOGRAPHICAL REFERENCES

1. W. W. Rostow, *The Stages of Economic Growth* (Cambridge, 1960), pp. 4–16.

2. C. Clark, *The Conditions of Economic Progress* (London, 1951), p. 401.

3. A. Bonné, *Studies in Economic Development* (London, 1957), p. 41.

4. R. Nurkse, *Some Aspects of Capital Accumulation in Underdeveloped Countries* (Cairo, 1952), p. 22.

5. A. M. Carr-Saunders, *World Population* (Oxford, 1936), p. 113.

6. Elaborated in A. B. Mountjoy, 'Vegetable Oils and Oilseed', *Geography* (1957), pp. 37–49.

R. Cohen, *The Economics of Agriculture* (Cambridge, 1959).

D. Warriner, *Land Reform and Development in the Middle East* (London, 1962) and *Land Reform in Principle and Practice* (London, 1969).

D. Grigg, *The Harsh Lands* (London, 1970).

5 Problems of industrialization

Economists recognize that an investment of the order of 12–15 per cent of the net national income is necessary if it is intended to diversify and advance a backward economy by the development of secondary and tertiary opportunities. The rate of return on such a degree of investment exceeds typical rates of population growth and permits of rising standards and cumulative returns. The maintenance of such a rate of investment allows the economy to move into the 'take-off' stage: the small snowball begins to roll. This is an over-simplification in that capital alone does not automatically engineer development for much depends on the qualities of the people: their ability and desire to learn and apply better methods of production, their enterprise, the removal of institutional obstructions and the provision of incentive to effort and investment. However, capital is a very necessary ingredient and the real nub of the matter lies in overcoming the complex problems standing in the way of attaining or bettering the 12 per cent-plus level. It is this ordering of economic progress by means of formulae, equations and interlocking of planning measures that is typical of the modern attack upon the problem of under-development. One reason for the necessity of the planned approach stems from the wide differences between the present developed lands in their early stages of growth and the present developing lands.

These extensive differences are often overlooked when development plans and theories are propounded, for the planning is generally based upon knowledge derived from the patterns of progress of the already developed lands. That we should draw upon accumulated experience is both natural and proper, but similarities here are only partial, differences must not be ignored. For example, to be told that England at the beginning of the nineteenth century and India today are examples of countries in the 'take-off' stage can be misleading.

Supposing an Englishman of those days met an Indian of these days and discussed their economic problems. The one takes off from London in a stage-coach, the other takes off in a Boeing 707 from New Delhi, and they reach Brighton—roughly speaking—at the same time. What common language of economic development can they talk, when they take off their coats and get down to it?[1]

Perhaps a fundamental difference to note is that industrial development in the pioneer countries such as Britain did not happen according to plan. The government did not ordain and design the country's industrialization, but rather a series of favourable factors and circumstances converged (expanding overseas trade, the growth of both men and institutions of commerce and credit, the surge of science and inventions becoming increasingly applied to a wide resource base). In short, in a bumbling haphazard way an industrial economy was evolved in Britain and took some eighty years over it. Such continental neighbours as Belgium, France and Germany gradually took the same path, their economic and social revolutions also gathered speed slowly and ran through several generations. In contrast, development in the present under-developed lands must be much more speedy and orderly. Advances are likely to come less from evolution within than as a result of government-sponsored imposition from without.

The earliest industrial countries had virtually no rivals: they were the first in the field and their gains were great and tended to become cumulative. The situation regarding overseas markets for manufactured goods is now very different for the state at present attempting to develop an industrial sector. However, the hard-won technical knowledge and scientific advances of developed countries are rapidly available to backward lands and at least from the point of view of technology there need be no long period of trial and error. Whether the human resources of the developing lands can be moulded into the forms and societies of the older industrialized countries and whether such patterns are necessary is more problematical. At any rate ideas and knowledge flow far more quickly around the world and, incidentally, money and its effects also move and fructify far more swiftly. Today there should not need to be the long gestation period of the nineteenth-century development pattern before economies are clear of the 'take-off' stage.

There are other very striking differences to be taken into account such as the very low standards of living and mental attitudes in most of the present developing lands. It is false to think of the masses in these lands as being at the stage and level of people in this country two hundred years ago. The present lot of the Indian *ryot*, Iraqi *fellah* and Paraguayan *peon* suggests a much closer analogy with the England of Domesday. The leap forward is to be immense and yet must be relatively sudden; time is no longer with the developing countries.

Finally, one of the greatest differences lies in the demographic structure. Populations in so many of the developing lands are larger and at a lower standard of living than in Western Europe in the early nineteenth century, also almost all now have a more rapid rate of population increase and a higher proportion of young workers. These differences have both advantages and disadvantages. On the positive side the labour of the dense and growing population offers a great resource for a developing and expanding industrial sector. The broad-based population pyramid of Britain in the nineteenth century provided a dynamic element in economic development; going hand in hand with increasing 'know-how' it fostered and more than supplied a steadily expanding demand, in addition to furnishing many millions for the newly developing lands overseas. Steadily improving agriculture, dispensing with labour, also contributed its quota to this design. In certain conditions, therefore, the vast labour resources found in many of the developing lands are a great economic asset and must be fully utilized.

However, on the negative side it must be remembered that humanity is capital-absorbing as well as being (by work) capital-forming. The vast masses inadequately employed in so many backward lands are a great handicap to capital formation, and the cost of providing services for large population increments may be crippling. To train, equip and absorb one individual into non-agricultural employment in Asia has been estimated at $1500, and this sum is in close accord with the estimated capital figure per new worker in India's second Five Year Plan.[2] Such a figure gives some indication of the enormous cost of programmes of industrialization to such populous countries as China and India, where massive populations totalling well over 1000 million are now expanding at an annual rate of well over 2 per cent. It has been found that in the early phases of planned development India cannot provide employment for the full increment to her population; it may be possible that with greater austerity imposed under Communist central planning that China might. India's second Five Year Plan, for example, managed to provide work for the equivalent of 80 per cent of new members to the labour force – the great mass of unemployed and under-employed remaining uncatered for. With the theoretical complementary advance in agriculture and the release of workers to non-agricultural employment the problem of the provision of capital assumes immense dimensions. Nothing like this was experienced in Western Europe; Britain's population in 1801 was only nine million and increasing by about 150 000 per annum (1·6 per cent per annum), but with a far broader-based economy and diversity of economic activity and no condition of agrarian over-population to compare with those of Egypt, India, Java, China and Japan today. The heavy annual increments to the labour force in these countries also serves to depress agricultural wage levels and to keep them low – part of the vicious circle of poverty which in turn impedes saving and the formation of capital.

THE PLACE OF CAPITAL

It is obvious that the developing countries are under-equipped with capital in relation to their populations and natural resources. It has been pointed out that circular forces – the 'vicious circle of poverty' – operate to constrict the formation and accumulation of capital by those countries.[3] In simplified form these forces and their effects are set out in Fig. 6, where it may be seen how the limitations and deficiencies imposed by poverty react upon the size of markets and capacity to save, and thus limit capital attraction and formation. Consequently traditional labour-intensive occupations continue, their low productivity being a cause of the prevailing poverty. To this depressing situation must be added the aggravation of heavily increasing populations laying increasing claims to the very limited supply of capital. The supply of capital has so often been stressed as the key to development and prosperity for under-developed lands, but the supply of unlimited capital will not in itself create development: skilled and willing hands are needed to turn the key to open the door. Professor Kuznets underlines this when he states 'the major capital stock of an industrially advanced country is not in its physical equipment; it is the body of knowledge amassed from tested findings and the capacity and training of the population to use this knowledge effectively'.[4] Capital is but one of a number of economic factors that combine with social, political and cultural forces in bringing about the changes inherent in development. It is an important factor and may be likened to a catalyst in its effects upon other factors.

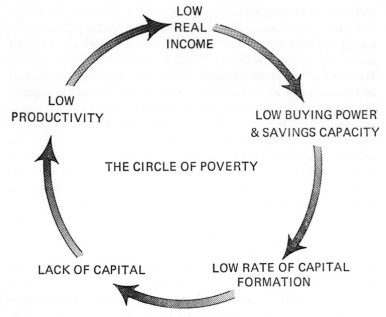

Fig. 6. The circle of poverty.

It is generally accepted that the application of capital is one of the conditions necessary for a breaking of the vicious circle of poverty. This implies the creation of conditions favourable to the internal formation of capital and to the attraction of external capital. It also implies a carefully assessed and integrated pattern of investment from which maximum advantage may accrue to all sectors of the economy and from which the necessary public utilities conducive to further growth are created or strengthened. The necessity for overall planning and therefore considerable governmental interest, scrutiny and even active participation has now come to be regarded as a normal feature of development whereas it was rare a century ago. There is no question of not being able to break the vicious circle of poverty. After all, the present developed lands were themselves once under-developed, and they have successfully taken the necessary steps. Although initially poor, a part of current income was deflected or set aside to create and augment a stock of capital.

In this country we gloss over the great poverty and dreadful working conditions in mills, mines and factories in the first century of our industrialization. The rich industrialists and mine owners may well have built their pseudo-Gothic mansions and given popularity to the term *nouveau riche*, but it was these shrewd hard-headed men who ploughed back much of their wealth into their enterprises and saw them expand, proliferate and fructify to an extent never before known. It is on the foundations they laid that Britain fought two great wars and founded her welfare state. Britain pulled herself up by her own bootstraps, for external sources of capital available to her were very limited. To an increasing degree her imitators and successors were helped by foreign investment and today this is an important potential source of capital for newly developing countries. Even so, the hardships, vicissitudes and sacrifices undergone in the course of industrialization by the present advanced countries are likely to be just as necessary and must be an accepted part of the process to be undergone by the developing lands. Development will not come without effort, hardship and sacrifices, no matter how much help may come from outside. Without the right social and political climate investment may be ineffective, but it may not even be attracted, for capital is cautious and will not venture where it may be ill-used.

PROBLEMS OF CAPITAL FORMATION

It is useful for planning purposes to have some idea of the productivity of capital, and the ratio of capital invested to resultant increase of output is frequently quoted (the capital: output ratio). Economists admit that this ratio is a very rough measure, especially in developing lands where data are scarce, but for planning purposes some such estimates are necessary. In an industrial country an investment of £100 may lead to an increase in the national income of £33 a year; the capital : output ratio thus being 3 : 1. At such a rate an annual net investment of 12 per cent of national income should result in an annual increase of about 4 per cent in the national income, figures that generally are typical of industrial countries. Estimates of likely coefficients in developing countries vary. India's first Five Year Plan was apparently based on a capital : output ratio of 3 : 1 and this in fact proved to be an under-estimate. Economists generally agree that in under-developed countries the marginal capital : output ratio is likely to be more of the order of 4:1.

Most developing countries with traditional economies save no more than 5–6 per cent of their net national incomes. To establish themselves in a position for 'take-off' into a fully developed economy requires an annual investment averaging 12–15 per cent of the net national income dependent upon the rate of increase of their populations. In broad terms this is the financial target to be arrived at. The low rate of capital formation in under-developed countries has barely been sufficient to keep pace with population growth. With a capital : output ratio of 4:1 the investment of 5 per cent of net national income would produce enough to sustain a population increase of about 1·25 per cent at the existing income level. If a higher rate of population increase pertains and if standards of living are to rise a far higher rate of investment is clearly necessary.

The general poverty of these countries means that the level of domestic saving is very low, the bulk of the population may have no productive savings, any nest-eggs possessed are usually in the form of gold rings, bracelets, jewellery. To persuade such peoples of the purpose, advantages and safety of such institutions as post office savings banks, thrift societies and insurance is a difficult and lengthy process. It is worth while, but is not likely to result in the saving of much more than 2 per cent of the net national income. An estimate of the value of privately owned gold in India is $3675 million. 'This is a large amount in absolute terms, being historical accumulation of stocks, but new hoarding is small . . . the role of gold as a savings medium in India is comparatively insignificant.'[5] A point worth noticing here is that a maldistributed national income (such as the United Kingdom's during the nineteenth century and today in those countries where land ownership still brings in disproportionate wealth) is far more favourable to saving and investment than one which is more evenly distributed. It favours more speedy development, although possibly at the expense of social unrest and dissatisfaction.

No nation should find it impossible to save 12 per cent of its national income given the will and strength of purpose to organize its affairs to that end. All too often under-developed lands are regarded as too poor to do this, yet frequently it will be found that 25–40 per cent of their national income is in the hands of a few thousand landlords who dissipate much of it in ostentatious living and convert a good deal into gold and jewellery. If this money went as taxes to the government for reinvestment, or as profits to industrialists to be ploughed back into business, there would be little difficulty in attaining a high rate of investment. Here, of course, is one of the underlying reasons for land reform measures as an initial step to development in so many poor countries.

It is clear that domestic saving can contribute only a very small part of the investment capital needed; much more should be forthcoming from the ploughing back of profits of existing undertakings. This form of self-capitalization is commonplace in industrial countries, indeed most firms' expansion depends upon reinvestment of undistributed profit although initial investment may have been from external sources. Thus a high level of profits and a population inculcated with the propensity to save, or an austere regime permitting the greatest proportion of reinvestment, would seem to be required. Taxation policies designed to absorb marginal income, whereby money going into circulation returns immediately to the government without creating big price increases, are favoured by those economists who point out that with such conditions a controlled inflation favours building up government capital. Developing lands notoriously have very low rates of taxation on marginal incomes and therefore much scope for such measures.

It is illuminating to examine briefly the cases of Japan and Russia to see the principal methods they adopted to obtain the necessary rate of investment for sustained and cumulative economic development. Japanese early development had some unusual facets. During the nineteenth century landowners and nobles were recompensed by the government which took over their duties and administrative functions. This led to many of these erstwhile landowners and feudal lords becoming capitalists, entering banking and interesting themselves in industrial developments; especially after 1880 when the government sold some of the factories it had built for pioneer development. These enterprises were supported by a virtual continuance of the former austere consumption pattern of the people. The semi-isolation of the Japanese at this time and the discipline of the people made this possible. It is estimated that before 1914 Japan saved and reinvested between 12 and 17 per cent of her national income. Little foreign capital entered Japan before 1920. These policies were fostered and supplemented by the government's taxation and subsidization measures.

Tsarist Russia similarly bought out the feudal landlords and the rents deflected from them became invested in commerce and industry. Banking institutions expanded during the latter part of the nineteenth century and foreign capital became attracted. Undoubtedly the early stages of the 'take-off' were accomplished before the 1917 Revolution. Under the subsequent Communist regime isolation from the high and rising consumption standards of developed countries has been a major factor in the economic development of the USSR, where rigid planning and control over personal liberty have become ruthlessly dedicated to economic progress. Where vested interests and institutional obstacles to growth can be swept aside, and where low consumption standards can be maintained, a high rate of capital formation is possible. Other features reinforcing the state capitalist advantage over the private capitalist are the taxation powers and monetary policies it can enforce. The critical 1930s saw tremendous inflation and rising profits which were transferred by taxation to the government. The result of all this has been one of the speediest rates of capital formation in the world, but it should be noticed that such a high rate is only possible where an iron curtain exists preventing free knowledge of the consumption standards elsewhere.

Development of foreign trade in many cases has played a substantial part in economic developments. National resources permitting export of primary products have helped to finance the import of machinery and equipment, and to pay interest on loans during the 'take-off' period. United States and Canadian grain, Australian wool, Swedish timber, Venezuelan oil provide such examples. However, as has been pointed out, conditions are changing and except for oil the demand for primary products lags behind the expansion of industry partly due to the greater use of synthetics and economies in the use of raw materials.

PROBLEMS OF CAPITAL ATTRACTION

Imported capital has played a large part in the economic development of many countries; cases where virtually all capital has been obtained from internal sources are not typical. Foreign investment very often plays a major part in establishing basic utilities necessary for the erection of the industrial superstructure. These enterprises, such as railway development, are far more costly than establishing individual manufacturing industries and require a long period of gestation before they become really fruitful ventures. Their presence, however, is generally indispensable for further industrial advance.

Foreign capital may be either government or agency controlled (such as loans from the World Bank) or investment by private enterprise. Previously, private investment, the expression of private foreign enterprise, was the largest overseas source of capital. Today the enormous demand for capital from the greater part of the world

struggling for economic advance is far greater than private investment alone can supply and the need of aid from public funds of the
advanced industrial countries has become accepted. Aid from the
rich countries to the poorer ones has gathered impetus from the
early 1960s. The United Nations Organization has repeatedly
pressed for greater generosity on the part of the donors and an
annual aid target of 1 per cent of GNP has been urged, but as yet
has rarely been attained. In the three years to March 1960 British
government assistance to overseas countries was £81 million,
£110 million and £138 million.[6] In 1969 British government assistance
to developing countries overseas was £211 million. Of this £179
million was bilateral (country to country aid) and £32 million was
multilateral aid (given through international agencies). Most of the
bilateral aid went to Commonwealth countries. Private overseas
investment in developing countries that year is put at about £156
million net. The joint figure for 1969 of £367 million represents about
0·9 per cent of the national income of the United Kingdom. Generally, grants are made to colonies and loans to independent members
of the Commonwealth, a pattern possibly reflecting the fact that the
poorer countries cannot attract all the private investment they need.
More recently, however, some of the independent countries of the
Commonwealth have been able to attract all the private investment
they desired. Capital more than ever has become a scarce resource
and needs to be attracted, wooed and cosseted. The global pattern
of aid in recent years is set out in Table 6. Total aid in real terms has
increased only moderately over the last decade, despite the fact that
the richer countries have been increasing their national wealth by
*c.*5 per cent per annum. Further, an increasing proportion of aid is
having to be used by the developing countries to repay past loans
or interest on them.

Foreign capital is rarely popular in overseas countries, especially
those which are or have been of colonial status. This arises partly
because of feelings of dependence and exploitation and also upon the
past pattern of private investment in these countries which concentrated almost entirely upon primary production and extractive
industries for export rather than upon industrial development
for a domestic market. This pattern, very typical of the nineteenth
century, reflected the poverty of the local domestic market as opposed
to the vigorously expanding markets for primary products and raw
materials in the industrialized countries. Private investment, after all,
is a reflection of market demand and this explains why so much of

Table 6: *Financial aid to developing countries, 1961–71*

(*US$ millions*)

	1961	1964	1967	1969	1970	1971
Government and agency aid	5647	5828	6772	7003	7841	8838
France	948	829	808	938	986	1131
W. Germany	559	399	504	433	641	802
United Kingdom	436	471	469	412	422	550
USA	3069	3272	3543	3183	3157	3392
Other countries	635	857	1448	2027	2635	2963
Private long-term capital	2362	2009	3896	6031	6408	7478
TOTAL	8009	7837	10 668	13 033	14 249	16 622

SOURCE: *United Nations Statistical Yearbook, 1972* (New York, 1973), table 198.

it prefers to be reinvested in remunerative enterprises in developed countries. Direct investment from the United States has shown a marked preference for Canada and West Europe and it should be noted that much of her heavy investment in developing lands since the Second World War has been in the oil industry.

It is surprising that so many developing countries, instead of extending inducements to private capital, create deterrents which frighten it away. Restrictions on transfer of profits or of capital, discriminatory taxation, exclusion from particular fields of investment, rules whereby a set (and often very high) proportion of local workers must be employed, immigration and import licence restrictions, the fear of arbitrary and ill-recompensed nationalization are all very real difficulties imposed by various countries and deterring the would-be foreign investor. Many developing countries are particularly sensitive to receiving aid with strings, and hypersensitive to anything resembling foreign interference; thus much of the capital supplied may not be used efficiently. Increasingly development projects are carefully vetted before international organizations lend capital, but it is still rare for the actual spending of the money to be overseen or controlled. Direct investment, whereby a foreign firm invests directly in its own subsidiary in a foreign country, is not likely to be misused or wasted for such investment issues from impartial examinations of commercial possibilities and not from any national or political considerations. A form of aid becoming increasingly fashionable is in tied loans, whereby countries or consortia offer the capital, and often arrange for the construction of distinct large-scale projects – such as a steel mill or a nuclear power station. Such projects are spectacular and can stand as monuments to the foreign power; the more numerous but less spectacular projects lacking glamour are often more difficult to finance and this may become increasingly so as the demand for capital goes on expanding.

The total foreign aid needed if India's fifth plan is to be carried out is about £2500 million over the five years. In the next few years, as more countries put development plans into effect, the total foreign capital needed will surpass this great sum many times. Countries and projects will be competing for a scarce resource and inducements rather than deterrents will be necessary, particularly where capital is needed for manufacturing industry. Whereas capital flows moderately well into mining and plantations and to some degree into utilities such as power, and port facilities, it tends initially to shun manufacturing, for here difficulties and risks may be greatest. This situation was noticeable in Egypt after the First World War; much foreign capital was available for financing commerce, land companies and mortgage banks but early Egyptian industry was less attractive and mainly had to be self-supporting. A big step forward was taken in 1920 with the establishment of the Misr Bank, one of its aims being to float Egyptian companies and to create a body of Egyptian shareholders. The capital and staff of this bank were entirely Egyptian and they promoted eight companies in the following ten years: several, however, having initial capital of only £10 000 or less. The difficulty of forming and attracting sufficient capital was a principal reason for the slow and halting early growth of manufacturing in Egypt, and the conditions then pertaining there are being faced today by other countries which have reached a similar phase of development.

The scarcity of capital, the great demand for it and the risks it must face combine to bring about high rates of interest which have come to be accepted by developing countries, but can be a heavy burden where large investments are involved. The prevalence of high interest rates, however, does help to attract capital from both internal and external sources and also induces the borrower to use available resources wisely. Whereas capital is dear, labour is usually cheap in under-developed lands and an interesting problem lies in the relative uses of the two resources. All too often advising experts have sought technical efficiency by heavy investment in labour-saving machinery whereas economic efficiency might suggest a far greater 'homespun' element using a greater amount of labour with a more restrained use of capital. This will be discussed in more detail later, here we may merely underline a further difference between industrialized and developing economies, that what is both technically and economically efficient in the one, where rates of interest are low and cost of labour high, may not apply in the other where reverse conditions pertain.

MARKETS AND BALANCED GROWTH

All discussion, investigation and planning of industrial development necessarily revolves around the potential market. To succeed industry must sell its wares, either at home or abroad. A feature common to all the under-developed lands is the smallness of the home market. This is the chief obstacle to economic development and reflects a number of factors, but mainly the low purchasing power of the bulk of the population. The national income of the Sudan, for example, has been estimated at about £200 million per annum or about £20 per head of the population. There is considerable maldistribution of this national income and the mass of the population receives much less than £20 per head per annum. Most of it is spent on basic essentials, particularly food and such items as kerosene, tobacco, cotton cloth (according to the *Yearbook of Labour Statistics*, samples from developing countries suggest that 60–65 per cent of expenditure is on food, compared with 41 per cent in developed countries). Inevitably demands are inelastic at such low real-income levels and there is virtually no effective demand for the products of manufacturing industry. The small market for manufactures is usually supplied by imports and the quantity required is often very marginal to the total output of the overseas suppliers – a few days' production, in fact, being enough to satisfy this small market for the year.

This problem is, of course, a part of the vicious circle already noticed: low buying power and low capacity to save result in both a small formation of capital and small investment. The small market offers no scope for the deployment of capital and economic advances: we are reminded of Adam Smith's thesis that 'the division of labour is limited by the extent of the market'. It is noticeable that even big concerns established in developing countries do not confine their activities to one market; they generally extend their activities into a number of widely different undertakings. An example is the United Africa Co. whose undertakings in West Africa prior to redeployment in the 1960s were concerned with oil palm, rubber and banana plantations, with trading in cocoa, cotton, groundnuts, palm oil, hides and skins and with the operation of timber mills, a river fleet and river services.

It follows that a successful expansion of manufacturing for the home market necessarily depends upon raising productivity in a wide range of activities, for the low level of real income is a reflection of low productivity. The downward spiral of poverty embodies a chain reaction, each negative factor being the cause of the succeeding negative factor. Myrdal has pointed out that even as there can be a downward spiral, so theoretically an upward one should be possible (e.g. less poverty = more food = better health = greater productivity) and in fact if developing lands wish to leave the 'traditional' economy of Rostow to essay the 'take-off' they must make the sacrifices necessary to reverse the direction of their spiral.[7] Opinions as to the methods of reversing the downward spiral vary, but the fact that all sectors of an economy are interlocked and react mutually upon each other leads to the view that investment and incentives to higher production cannot be successful if applied only to one or two industrial (or agricultural) projects, but need to be applied judiciously to a wide range of activities.

If capital is invested in an industrial plant, machinery installed and workers trained, a far greater output per worker may be expected and the greater productivity should bring greater real income to them; but if in the rest of the economy there is no increase in productivity, and therefore buying power, the newly produced goods will lack a market. Much of the enhanced income of the workers will be spent on food, clothing and then a range of other goods; it would be absurd to expect them to spend their greater wealth in buying their own products. Under these conditions such an industrial activity would seem doomed, for the output of any single industry cannot create its own demand. But if simultaneous investment is made in a wide range of carefully selected agricultural projects, utilities and manufactures, the dissipation of the enhanced productivity and real wealth can make an impact and a wider market is achieved. This theory is often referred to as that of 'balanced growth' and rests upon the well-known fact of interrelation of activities whereby the workers in each, now working productively, play their part in consuming goods from the other expanding enterprises.[8] Thus productivity increases and markets can begin to expand and more capital is both formed and attracted.

The two main problems that are appearing as this theory becomes put into practice are those of co-ordination (for massive interdependence is the essence of the exercise) and the length of time, perhaps two or three decades, necessary for momentum to be built up for the 'take-off'.[9] An alternative path by 'unbalanced growth' has been propounded by Professor Hirschman. He bases his theory upon the varying degrees of complementarity between particular groups of industries.[10] The balanced growth theory aims at pushing forward on all fronts, in effect assuming that complementarities are equal. Hirschman suggests a concentration upon those industries where interdependence is most marked. He feels that dynamic development may be more rapid if some groups of industries become pace-setters for others. This theory is now being applied in southern Italy, the most under-developed region within the Common Market countries. Two 'poles of development' are being created at Bari and Taranto by the establishment of nine mechanical engineering industries. They in turn require the establishment of thirty auxiliary plants concerned with repairs, tooling, foundry-work, gear-cutting, pressing, moulding and galvanizing. These, and the infra-structure established for them, are expected to promote the growth of allied and service industries and to provide non-agricultural jobs so much needed throughout the Italian south.[11] It must not be thought that these theories apply solely to industrial establishments, but to all sections of the economy including public utilities, upon which many developing industries will depend, and especially upon agriculture. Although this book lays stress upon industrial development, the complementary position of developing agriculture must always be kept in mind. Improvements in agriculture necessarily should go hand in hand with industrial expansion, as has been shown in the history of the more advanced countries. India's first Five Year Plan led to an increase in the national income of 18 per cent, most of this being due to greater investment in and productivity from agriculture. In the decade 1951–61 industrial production in India grew by 120 per cent but her vast agricultural output grew also by 40 per cent, and during this period twenty million acres more land came under irrigation. Thus investment in agriculture – in irrigation, fertilizers, plant breeding, etc., occasionally also associated with land reform (as in

India, Egypt and Syria) – is generally to be expected as development gets under way. There are of course some developing countries where land is plentiful but inadequately used and where agricultural developments should in any case be paramount over the development of an industrial sector.

Planned investment in agriculture and manufacturing industry rests upon two things, the outlook, adaptability and desire to advance on the part of the people and therefore their acceptance of, and co-operation in, the inevitable changes, and the presence of the very necessary utilities and services upon which manufacturing industries rely: such facilities as transport, electricity, water, banking and insurance. These features of an economy, both human and material, usually develop slowly and eventually create a springboard from which an economy can take off. Today, when time is limited, the development of utilities and education and training of the people – precondition factors – are built into general development plans and may absorb the bulk of investment in early years and apparently give little return. These conditions differ considerably from those of the advanced countries: they require close and de-tailed planning and co-ordination and have necessarily become undertaken by governments.

For purposes of simplicity industrial development for the home market has been isolated and considered but it must be realized that with the majority of present developing countries, even with aims of balanced growth and selected investment injections, the home market although enlarging will be relatively small and cannot be expected to grow very rapidly in the early stages. One reason here is that government will deflect much of the early fruits of develop-ment from the people in the interests of reinvestment and the furthering of development, consequently with discipline and aus-terity their increase in purchasing power will be controlled. Thus it is possible to foresee a sated home market, the growth of manufac-turing industry retarded and establishments remaining stunted, denied economies of scale and cheaper production. One answer to this would seem to be a vigorous search for export markets. In finding and developing such a market many difficulties have to be overcome. Much depends upon the nature of resources available and the character of the growing industrial production, for the world market for some goods such as industrial equipment, electrical goods and vehicles expands steadily, but for other goods, such as railway equipment, textiles and clothing, it grows much more slowly and these goods are much more difficult to sell by newcomers to the market. One advantage these countries are likely to have is low cost of production stemming principally from low wages. If wages are low enough and the goods otherwise satisfactory, export markets may be obtained as Japan and Hong Kong have shown.

The foregoing may be examined from a different viewpoint if we think in terms of food and population. As was pointed out in Chapter 1, the employment of more and more people in secondary and tertiary activities does not produce more food but may increase the demand relative to the supply. In countries where population is in excess of agricultural resources it is imperative to export manufactures surplus to the home market if full employment is to be both attained and retained and food and raw materials imported. This is the familiar situation of Britain and Japan but it is also becoming true of India and Egypt, and will become true of many other developing countries in the next few decades.

THE POSITION OF GOVERNMENTS: THE NEED FOR PLANNING

Although it is not true that all the present advanced countries developed mainly as a result of private initiative, certainly the richest countries have done so. Their governments played only indirect roles in the unexpected, unpredictable, pioneer development of their economies. It may well be that in the pioneer period of innovation *laissez faire* was the only sensible policy. These economies developed slowly and almost by trial and error. Japan and Russia provide examples of governmental interest in, and furthering of, economic development, but here the economic well-being of their population was secondary to increasing the power of the state. The situation in the post-war world is much changed. Policies of economic growth to combat poverty and ignorance are accepted as prime objectives by many governments of developing countries. With a conscience awake in the advanced countries and a growing awareness of their poverty and lack of opportunity among the developing countries and with the mounting rate of population increase, it has come to be regarded by all that the swiftest way to economic development is necessarily by means of definite economic planning: a duty to be performed by the state.

Not only in the preparation of a plan, but also in its initial carry-ing out, it has come to be recognized that the government has to take over many of the roles and functions that are the realm of private business in developed countries. For example, many necessary early investments are unlikely to be profitable for a considerable period – it is in fact necessary to create many facilities to provide external economies for industries yet to be attracted. Had such investments been profitable private entrepreneurs would already have made them: as it is they are typical and essential measures of the precondition period. Thus we find the state setting out to do, as it were artificially in a short period, what has come to be regarded almost as natural growth over a long period in the advanced countries.

The plans are aimed at increasing a country's productive powers and attracting and forming the necessary capital for increased investment. A central authority is needed to determine total capital needs and to allocate proportions to various projects, to determine the order of priority of undertakings whereby there is the early creation of facilities for external economies to further and make remunerative succeeding projects, to sustain and develop agriculture, to educate and train the labour force, to inculcate among the population the acceptance of change, of new ideas and methods and to foster the will and determination to make the sacrifices necessary for ultimate success. The new role of governments in under-developed lands and the preparation and publicizing of plans sometimes creates certain misconceptions. Outside the iron curtain private investment and enterprise still has a large and, as economies move forward, a growing part to play. Nor must rigidity be considered synonymous with planning, for frequently the plan is but a series of guide posts to help departments and sections of the economy to travel the shortest road to the desired destination.

BIBLIOGRAPHICAL REFERENCES

1. M. Ionides, Letter to *The Economist* (20 February 1960).

2. United Nations Economic Committee for Asia and the Far East, *Economic Bulletin for Asia and the Far East*, vol. X (1959), pp. 33–45.

3. R. Nurkse, *Some Aspects of Capital Accumulation in Under-developed Countries* (Cairo, 1952), p. 1.

4. Quoted in United Nations, *Processes and Problems of Industrialization in Under-developed Countries* (New York, 1955), p. 5.

5. A. G. Chandavarka, 'The Nature and Effects of Gold Hoarding in Under-developed Economies', *Oxford Economic Papers* (1961), p. 138.

6. H.M. Stationery Office, *Assistance from the United Kingdom for Overseas Development*, Cmnd. 974 (1960).

7. G. Myrdal, *Economic Theory and Under-developed Regions* (London, 1957), p. 12.

8. P. T. Bauer and B. S. Yamey, *The Economics of Under-developed Countries* (Cambridge, 1959), p. 247.

9. H. Myint, *The Economics of the Developing Countries* (London, 1964), ch. 7.

10. A. O. Hirschman, *The Strategy of Economic Development* (New Haven, 1960), pp. 50–119.

11. A. B. Mountjoy, 'Planning and Industrial Developments in Apulia', *Geography* (1966), pp. 376–80.

I. K. D. Little and J. M. Clifford, *International Aid* (London, 1965).

L. B. Pearson, *Partners in Development* (London, 1969).

6 Environmental and human problems

Discussion of world development and under-development invariably is in the context of national units, since statistical data are available on a national basis over much of the world. In a sense this is a generalization and a simplification, in that within any country some regions will be developing more rapidly than others, which may even be stagnating (northern and southern Italy come to mind, or even south and mid-Wales). Myrdal has pointed out that as a general rule the poorer the country the greater the regional inequalities, for poor countries can spend little on public utilities, school and medical services and most parts of such countries remain backward, contrasting greatly with the few developed areas, such as near the ports where disadvantages to development are less severe. It is probably true to say that economists are more interested at the national level than are geographers, who are much more concerned with analysing and explaining local differentiation and the spatial pattern of development and under-development. It is at what might be termed the regional level that the role played by environment in association with economic, social and political factors is most readily discernible, and at this level economic geographers are finding a wide and fruitful field for investigation and analysis. At national level because of the very diversity of the component parts of most countries the weight of environmental factors is more difficult to isolate and assess. Such factors include size, position and degree of accessibility to major trade routes, climate, vegetation, topography and natural resources.

Geographical size of a country is not of great significance in itself, but in relation to population size may have a bearing upon the size of the market. There is, of course, no correlation between size of country and size of population and a wide range of variations may be discerned. It is probable, however, that the larger a country the greater the amount and diversity of its endowment of natural resources, the greater the range of its climates and variations of topography, land and water and, consequently, a greater potential for development and the support of a large population. These are, however, only possibilities and we have seen that development depends upon much more than resource endowment. A country of large size, however, has certain economic advantages over smaller countries that stem essentially from economies of scale. Costs of administration, defence, communications and basic utilities do not increase proportionately with size and generally bear more heavily upon the small country. On the other hand, small countries having smaller and more closely-knit populations possess greater flexibility and adaptability for social changes concomitant with advancing technology and economic growth.

CLIMATE AND MAN

Climate is one of the most outstanding geographical factors bearing upon economic development. The influence of climate on man, is, of course, all-pervasive: it is the predominant factor influencing the growth and distribution of plants; together with vegetation it strongly influences soil characteristics; it plays a part in the moulding of the surface features of the landscape. On man himself climate has both physiological and psychological effects, and influences pests and diseases that prey upon him. From the point of view of large-scale human settlement, the three negative climatic zones are the polar, tropical desert and the high mountain (where terrain, too, plays a major part). Here the rigour and severity of climate demonstrate an omnipotence over the landscape that is unlikely ever to be challenged on any great scale by man. The only economic activities here are local and specialized, such as operating oil wells and mineral concessions; natural circumstances inhibit settlement and economic development. The distribution of man over the globe is remarkably uneven, but the majority of mankind is to be found in two climatic belts: the temperate cyclonic and the tropical monsoon. The warm humid climates of the tropical monsoon areas are conducive to great fertility of both vegetation and humans, but it is in the more stimulating cooler and variable climate of the temperate cyclonic zone that the greatest economic development has taken place. The bulk of the under-developed countries lie in tropical latitudes and a number of others are in cold climates.

Possible relationships between climate and man, as manifest in his works and the progress of civilization, have interested numerous scientists and evoked a considerable literature. It is possible that the biologists' theory that a combination of certain conditions produce the finest stocks of plant and animal life can also be applied to human beings. Ellsworth Huntington has stressed the importance of climate in this connection, relating the past movement of leadership of the civilized world to past changes in climate.[1] His approach may err in being too enthusiastically deterministic and a number of his arguments have since been refuted. It seems likely that changing leadership of the civilized world, reflecting successive stages in the upward movement of civilization, has resulted from man's growing means of ameliorating the effects of climate and weather by clothing, housing and firing. This has permitted a gradual shift to cooler, variable and more stimulating areas where the greatest mental and physical vigour is possible. Markham has postulated that the ideal climate, where men can work hardest and with greatest efficiency, is where the daily temperature is between 60° and 76°F with a moderate humidity (say 40–70 per cent).[2] Dependent upon the amount and nature of clothing worn these constitute ideal indoor (or factory) conditions. Outdoor ideals are harder to assess owing to greater air movement and usually brisker activities, but in general the same band of temperature and humidity seems acceptable.

It follows that annual average temperatures of 70°F or slightly greater were conducive to the rise of early civilizations; the tendency to move northwards came with developments in spinning and the weaving of clothing and the provisions of means of heating by such inventions as the hypocaust, fireplace and chimney. Upper Egypt, Sumeria, India, Babylon and Assyria may be related to the 70°F annual isotherm. Greece and Rome show the first major move from it with the growing knowledge of house heating. After the fifteenth century improvements in housing materials and heating methods, appliances and fuels brought about a shift of emphasis northwards and to the coal-possessing countries. There, man's energy was no longer expended in surviving the winter cold, the mitigation of winter climate permitted civilization in a stimulating cool winter region, allowed indoor activities and brought to prominence coal. From a source of fuel coal also came to be a source of power and lifted Western civilization far ahead of its predecessors, until Europe and the white man assumed mastery over all the continents. It will be noticed that early civilization did not move to hotter, wetter zones; man has always found it easier to warm and dry air than to cool it,

D

and hotter, wetter climates are far less conducive to mental and physical energy and activity.

The conditions affecting man's efficiency in the tropics stem mainly from the heat and moisture. The human body maintains a constant body temperature of about 98·4°F. In health there is little variation from this figure and this is obtained by a physiological mechanism which maintains a balance between heat production and heat loss through the blood circulation, respiration, and secretion by sweat glands. Comfort is obtained at relatively high temperatures by an acceleration in the loss of body heat. Such heat is lost by radiation, conduction and evaporation; the rate and mode being influenced by temperature, humidity and velocity of the air and by the individual's activity. Dry heat may be resisted at very high temperatures – blast-furnace men work in temperatures approaching boiling-point – mainly by surface evaporation via the sweat glands. Moist heat presents a more serious set of problems for under hot, moist conditions loss of heat by the customary mechanisms is far more difficult. Hot moist air cannot take up much more moisture yet the heat makes the body perspire readily. If body heat is not dissipated, lethargy, weakness, spells of dizziness and a sense of depression characterize the onset of heatstroke, conditions reached when the wet bulb temperature passes 85°F. On the other hand, warm but very dry air is generally considered less comfortable and less healthy than air of moderate humidity, for dry air irritates the mucous membranes of throat and nose, favours respiratory disorders and leads to sleeplessness and nervous irritability.

It is generally held that the monotony of weather in parts of the tropics is responsible for much ill-health and depression, in that under such conditions the body's adaptability to change is reduced so that changes considered small in a variable climate have serious effects. Colds and chills are common in the tropics and the mortality rate from pneumonia is high. Knowledge of long-term effects of tropical climate is still inadequate and much of the present body of knowledge has been accumulated by studying climatic effects on the white man in the tropics rather than on the indigenous peoples. Yet, broadly, it seems that humans, whatever the colour of their skins are made the same way and react similarly to climatic stimuli. The black man's skin absorbs more solar heat than the white man's, but in compensation he has more sweat glands and he is also better protected against any damaging action of ultra-violet rays. In all humans it is thought that the reactions to warm conditions – a slight lowering of blood pressure from the suffusion of the capillaries and reduction of the blood viscosity ('the tropics thin one's blood') – while allowing of greater sweat volume generally reduce resistance to infection and pave the way for digestive and gastric disorders.

Although it is possible by means of attention to clothing, diet, exercise and hygiene to keep in good health in warm climates, the physical disadvantages of such climates compared with the 'ideal' cooler and more variable climates remain. There is substantial evidence of the poor productivity of much tropical labour owing to diseases and ill-health, particularly intestinal disorders and worm diseases which debilitate the body and lower output, but additionally tropical climates do not favour muscular activity which generates much body heat and discomfort and induces a disinclination to work. Estate records and observation suggest that agricultural workers in the tropics put in only twenty to thirty hours' work a week, and most of this in the early morning and in the cool of the evening. It has been estimated that, other things being equal, dockers in the Queensland port of Townsville accomplish 5 to 10 per cent less work than dockers at Brisbane, nine degrees to the south, and they do about 11 per cent more work in the cool season than in the hot. Long periods of sustained physical labour cannot be expected. One is led to the conclusion that labour in the tropics is unlikely to be as efficient as in temperate areas and that it will be more costly to maintain it at any reasonable level of efficiency.

Economic development in lower latitudes, however, demands more than mere physical labour and it is significant that there is a strong body of opinion that the warm wet climates are also inimical to sustained mental work. An investigation in Queensland before the last war drew attention to great fatigue and inertia experienced among professional people and clerks. Among psychological disturbances related to tropical climate a study group of the American Council on Foreign Relations particularly cited loss of mental initiative and the general need for higher concentration to perform a given task.[3] Part of the adaptation to warmer and moister climatic conditions is a more leisurely tempo of life and perhaps a greater tinge of fatalism, the *mañana* outlook so exasperating to the Occidental, who has created a civilization in which activity and making provision for the future hold a high place and derive from the demands imposed by cold winters. Tropical climates give less urgency and less value to these habits and the enthusiasm for planning, but procrastination in execution, is well known. Chaudhuri in his *A Passage to England*, underlines this aspect:

> The old British official in his sola topee could not escape the heat, and by bringing about a psychological adaptation it endowed him with a sense of the possible which was almost the same as wisdom. But in the artificial cool of the air-conditioned room the Indian and his Occidental friends alike acquire the habit of reckoning without the host. . . . For the Indian minister or official the mere discussion of his plans with an Occidental in an air-conditioned room is equivalent to execution. . . . In India the mirages of the mind are produced by coolness.[4]

It is true that the last twenty years have seen great advances in air-conditioning so that, for example, Lancashire air conditions may be simulated in textile mills elsewhere, but these aids are not for the masses: it is a very localized control of climate and ceases on the doorstep. It is an aid to efficiency under warm conditions, especially in factories, but should not be overrated.

CLIMATE AND TRANSPORT

Accessibility and adequate transport facilities are inherent needs of developing industries. Means of transport in most tropical countries are usually limited in scope and expensive in operation. While it is true that present limited transport nets primarily reflect existing low levels of development, environmental difficulties (and particularly those of climate) exert substantial restraining effects. The range of variation of relief and climate in the tropics is very great and here only general features, but of wide application, will be considered. In many cases development of roads and railways has either been in response to haphazard demand generated by successful mining ventures or has in itself created conditions where large-scale production for export becomes a worthwhile proposition. Examples are the railway line from Lagos to the tin mines on the Bauchi plateau of Nigeria and the transcontinental line through the copper belt of Central Africa. The development of the beef-cattle industry in the Argentine and the growth of cocoa farming in the Gold Coast owe much to the construction of the railway lines, while commercial cotton growing in Uganda and coffee production in Kenya followed the construction of the Mombasa–Kisumu railway in 1902. In that year the line carried 13 000 tons of freight and 73 000 passengers. In 1950 it dealt with two million tons of freight and three million passengers.

The result, clearly to be seen in tropical Africa, is the lack of a railway net, but instead the presence of a series of disconnected lines striking inland from the ports. It is true that a growing road system feeds and supplements these lines until a rudimentary transport net appears, but the mesh is remarkably coarse when judged by standards of developed countries. In tropical Africa there are 14 805 miles of railway serving an area of over five million sq. miles. In Britain 51 000 miles of railway serve 88 000 sq. miles. Appreciable areas even with known resources may remain undeveloped owing to inaccessibility where the cost of providing transport facilities is in excess of the likely return, as is the case with a number of known mineral deposits in the Brazilian interior or iron ore at Mount Patti near Lokoja in Nigeria. One reason for this lies in the very great size of some of the territories and the great distances involved, often necessitating the crossing of large unproductive areas. The copper belt of Zambia has been described as 'an industrialized oasis in a desert of unproductiveness', for at least 500 miles around there is relatively little settlement or even agriculture.[5] Most of the refined ore has had to travel a single-track line for 1450 miles to Beira in Mozambique (practically the distance from Paris to Moscow). The trade is ill-balanced, return freight being far less than out-going ores and tobacco. Actual cost of construction over such distances is heavy – sometimes even ballast has to be brought great distances – while frequent use of wood for fuel reduces efficiency and raises operating costs. Locomotives of the East African railways have to operate in a temperature range of 35°–100°F, at altitudes ranging from sea-level to over 9000 feet, in tropical rainstorms and in dusty semi-desert conditions.

Although railways are also affected, it is roads that suffer most from tropical weather. The majority of roads in monsoon Asia, Africa and South America are unsurfaced: pot-holes, deep furrows and quagmires come with the rainy season, embankments and bridges on railway tracks may be washed away, while in the dry season corrugations on the surface and choking dust render unpleasant all movement by road and may even render difficult the supply of water for locomotives. The provision of bitumen-surfaced all-weather roads is costly and therefore slow: in Zambia even dirt roads cost £1000 per mile to construct. On the credit side waterways with which many tropical countries are endowed must be recognized, they persist in many places traditionally as slow but relatively cheap media of movement and transport. However, they too offer obstacles and difficulties such as rapids and falls, seasonal changes of volume affecting both depth and current velocity, and for full development and integration into national transport nets considerable expenditure on dredging, bypasses to rapids, flood control, wharf and handling facilities is to be expected. In short, the provision of transport facilities on a considerable scale is recognized as a prerequisite of economic development and in tropical areas costs and difficulties involved will be far heavier than in developed countries, in large measure due to limitations and obstacles of the environment.

UTILITIES AND SERVICES

The provision of public utilities and services in countries aspiring to industry is fundamental and costly. Often in the past these have been painstakingly built up over a long period, but now a swifter pace is becoming essential. Not only are roads, railways, port facilities, telephones and power and water supplies needed but also law and order, the provision of hospitals and health measures, and education. Investment in these measures for a long period is likely to exceed investment in manufacturing. The capital : output ratio is very high in such an investment, for initially the return is often low, one is putting one's faith and money in future usefulness (as in the case of the Kenya–Uganda railway quoted above). Industries cannot develop without them and although private capital has been available for these relatively 'safe' investments, often having monopolist attributes, increasingly governments must pay a large share in their finance. This has always been so: in the United States for example the Erie Canal was constructed by the New York State legislature, the TVA, a major power producer, was a Federal project, and even the great transcontinental railway nets received Federal subsidy in the guise of land grants. There is no short cut to the creation of these foundations (or infra-structure) which can absorb vast amounts of development capital. Forty-two per cent of India's planned expenditure under her first four Five Year Plans was allocated to power, transport and education, while only 19 per cent was allocated to industry and mining.

Development of utilities can never be countrywide and initially in a developing country may well be very limited in spatial distribution. The limitations thus imposed upon location of industrial establishments tend to reinforce a natural gregariousness of many industries. The development of industrial complexes in richer countries is traceable to a number of factors offering locational advantages to the component establishments. Generally the more industries that are located in a given area the greater the external economies that become possible. Many industries are closely related using similar raw materials or component parts, others may make the component parts. For example, a furniture-making industrial area is likely to include factories making springs, latex rubber, upholstery fabrics, castors, glue and resins as well as those making furniture. Cardboard container and wrapper factories, and then printing establishments, may be attracted to sites near paper mills. Examples in the engineering industry are even greater. Light industries attach themselves where labour and markets are available. In short, natural centripetal tendency may be considerably reinforced if lack of utilities discourages location elsewhere.

In many densely populated developing countries this tendency may conflict with official ideas. A widespread dissemination of industrial establishments might seem a more direct and healthier method of relieving rural under-employment: a physical spread of manufacture rather than a fiscal spread of its rewards. It might be suggested that here lie paths of industrial development differing from those of the developed lands but eminently applicable to meeting the major problems of developing countries. In fact, this overall development within a country is impossible if normal locational forces are allowed free play. Latitude in locational decisions is much restricted, not merely by limitation of utilities and services but in many cases by the character and availability of raw materials. An iron and steel plant within Basilicata (Lucania), south Italy, might bring substantial benefit to the impoverished rural population, but such a situation remote from the heavy and bulky raw materials, fuel and markets is doubtful if iron and steel are to be produced at competitive prices. Careful cost studies are essential in deciding the locations of such heavy basic industries: high costs here, emanating from faulty or arbitrary location, can leave an impress on the whole economy. An essential requirement in the developing countries whose populations have limited purchasing power is that production costs and selling price should be low, thus normal locational forces will have to be respected. A conjunction of circumstances suggests that irrespective of non-economic or social ideals a pattern of regional specialization will inevitably appear as secondary activities increase. Certain manufactures orientated to market and but loosely tied by raw material needs may show a countrywide distribution. Such establishments are likely to be small, serving only a limited and local market. All in all, a close relationship to existing major urban centres is to be expected (where basic utilities and some manufacturing industry are already likely to be available).

Limited provision of utilities and services will be an important contributive factor to such a growth pattern as conditions in India readily show:

> Any city of less than 100000 population and many cities above this population will have totally inadequate public services. The streets are of mud and become running sewers during the monsoon. Water supply may be inadequate and polluted. Electrical services will be irregular. Delivery of inbound materials from the nearest rail junction may take days or weeks, and the assignment of outbound empties is uncertain. Mail and telegraph services will be regular, if slow, but telephone service will be most difficult. Visiting salesmen and customers may get there only with journeys of many hours on uncomfortable trains. . . . Their contact with competitors, customers, supplies and the market place in general will be greatly impaired.[6]

It is evident that the largest metropolitan centres in such developing lands have notable advantages that will accelerate their further growth despite policies that may favour more widely disseminated industrial growth. It may well be that the 'megalopolis' tendency in warmer latitudes has scarcely yet begun, despite significant increase in the last decade.

There are undoubted economic and social advantages possible from increasing urbanization, but the views of those attempting to limit it by 'planning' new industry into rural and small town locations should be appreciated. There is a natural reaction against the overcrowded slum conditions and squalor to be found in every city; there is the political fear of a growing urban proletariat; the realization of inevitable social and cultural changes divorced from tradition bred of rural forebears. Above this there is the realization that there is a limit to economies of scale in relation to economic and urban growth. Cities can become too big for economic efficiency; their arteries can become so congested that they can no longer function and in the process maximum discomfort, nervous strain and artificial way of life is produced. Already Bombay, Calcutta, Cairo, São Paulo and Peking have over five million people each, and Djakarta, Rio de Janeiro and Karachi over four million.

RESOURCE PROBLEMS: RAW MATERIALS

It was pointed out earlier that the economic prospects of a country cannot be gauged solely by cataloguing its known natural resources. This method may suggest potentiality as now in the case of Brazil and until recently China, but resources in themselves are valueless unless they harmonize with a complex network of other economic and social factors. Resources are given value by the application of capital, labour and technical skills. Such application hinges upon the further factor of economic accessibility, itself dependent upon available markets which in turn involve consideration of cost : price ratios and degrees of competition. It is certainly wrong to dismiss the resource (including energy) base as unimportant, but neither is it paramount. In the modern world possibilities of industrialization do not hinge upon possession or non-possession of raw material resources; in any case virtually all countries in the world possess some potential or actual agricultural and mineral resources (even the sands of Arabia and the Sahara cloak rich oil deposits). The resource pattern, while not determining whether or not industry shall exist, does exert influence upon the character and intensity of any development that may occur.

In general terms the presence and proximity of iron ore and coal, from the resource point of view, facilitated the growth of great iron (and later steel) industries in Britain, Germany and the eastern United States. Britain's early start and gathering momentum soon led to the import of higher quality foreign ore; the local raw material lost much significance and this was reflected in locational readjustments of the industry. This industry is basic to modern civilization; it ramifies into a great range of constructional, transport and engineering activities and with its growing links with chemicals and the power industries makes possible an enormous and diverse industrial superstructure. The case of Britain also demonstrates the decreasing significance of indigenous resources once development is under way and when a growing body of capital, skill, technical knowledge, entrepreneurial experience and wide overseas markets become deployed.

Of a totally different character is the industrial pattern within Switzerland, where two-thirds of the country is mountainous; where there are no mineral resources, no coal, iron and oil, but sources of hydraulic energy, scenic beauty and an advantageous position astride international routeways. Switzerland is a small country, her labour force and domestic market are small and, except for a limited range of agricultural products, raw materials have to be imported. These problems are overcome by her concentration on high-quality goods for export markets, and by the application of highly skilled labour and much capital. Switzerland is denied the customary bases of heavy industry and instead concentrates on manufacturing industry. To export, however, she must overcome competition from manufactures of richer countries holding the advantages denied her: they can mass-produce standard articles for their large markets far more cheaply than could Switzerland. Consequently the Swiss find it pays to concentrate on manufactures where precision and quality predominate and put emphasis upon the selective rather than the mass market.

Japan has had to overcome different problems. She has a wider endowment of resources than Switzerland, possessing some coal (but unsuitable for coking purposes), limited supplies of oil, some hydraulic energy, iron ore of poor quality, some copper, sulphur and raw silk. Her manner of use of these materials has been greatly influenced by her acute population problem. Like Switzerland she must export, both in order to support her population and pay for the massive imports of raw materials needed to supplement domestic supplies. Her labour costs are far lower than Switzerland's and other developed countries and, being associated with a high level of efficiency, permit relatively low-cost production. This has facilitated the growth of a wide industrial structure including a base of heavy industry, despite the necessity of importing coking coal, iron ore, non-ferrous metals, crude oil and other raw materials.

Unlike Switzerland, Japan provides exports for the highly competitive cheap mass markets, but in order to maintain, if not improve, existing standards of living in the face of swiftly growing numbers, native skills are being turned increasingly to the 'Swiss type' of product – articles requiring little raw material but much investment of capital and skilled labour, such as in high-quality precision camera and lens manufacture.[7] Japan also combats her shortage of certain raw materials by obtaining concessions and commercial control of supplies in India and crude oil concessions beneath coastal waters in the Persian Gulf: measures generally impossible to poorer countries.

Not all natural resources available for transmutation into raw materials offer equal advantages to newly industrializing countries. Deposits of iron ore and coal might be considered superior to an endowment for agricultural raw materials only. The foregoing examples suggests reasons for this. Metallurgical industries being basic to a wide and comprehensive industrial superstructure have a notable advantage, and at the same time it must be recognized that there is a greater world demand for metal manufactures than for, say, textiles or boots and shoes. During the first half of the twentieth century international trade in metal manufactures increased from 31 per cent to 56 per cent of world trade in manufactures, while trade in other commodities increased far more slowly or even declined. Developing countries lacking bases for metallurgical industries must face the problem of competition among themselves for a share of a declining trade in the simple metal goods and in manufactures based on agricultural raw materials.

THE FUTURE SUPPLY OF RAW MATERIALS

The adequacy of the supply of raw materials under conditions of increasing world industrialization presents a further problem, particularly to the poorer nations. A shortage of a range of raw materials, especially minerals (which unlike agricultural products are non-renewable), is much feared. Development and the raising of standards of living create growing demand for capital and consumer goods and thereby increase the world demand for raw materials. So far the rapid increase of raw material consumption reflects the growing wealth of the already developed countries. The United States of America, with less than a fifteenth of the world's population, already consumes about half the non-Communist world's supply of principal minerals and all but a tiny fraction of the remainder are used by the other developed countries; the developing lands holding over two-thirds of the world's population use only 6 per cent of these raw materials.

The growing problem of raw material consumption was given publicity in the United States in 1952 by the report of the President's Materials Policy Commission (better known as the Paley Report). This revealed that in the last half-century the tremendous advance in the standard of living in the United States of America saw mineral consumption increase eight times, that of fuel and energy twelve times and the consumption of paper fourteen times while the population merely doubled. Truly the United States' appetite has become gargantuan. It is of great significance that whereas up to thirty years ago the United States produced rather more than the materials she required, by 1950 there was a 10 per cent deficit. The Report suggests that the demand over the next generation will be double that consumed by the last generation. The United States will be purchasing more and more of these materials from world markets on an ever-increasing scale and in addition there will be growing demand from the other developed countries experiencing fast rising standards of living. The Report made estimates of future supplies on the assumption of the finality of the then known reserves (Table 7).

Table 7: *Estimated years of supply of important metals*

Metal	Years of supply at rate of consumption in	
	1950	*1975*
Iron ore (probable)	200	150
(potential)	1200	740
Bauxite	300	70
Copper	80	50
Lead	25	15
Zinc	30	20
Tin	35	25
Nickel	120	60
Tungsten (non-Communist countries only)	40	17

SOURCE: US Government, *Resources for Freedom*, vol. II, 1952.

Our endowment of minerals is limited to what exists in the earth's crust. There is an abundance of constructional materials (stone, clay, sand and cement) and no immediate shortage of the principal chemical materials is envisaged. The two most important metals, iron and aluminium, form 5 per cent and 8 per cent of the earth's crust respectively and should last man for hundreds of years. Known resources of non-ferrous metals valuable for alloys, coatings and conductors, however, are much smaller. The figures in Table 7 suggest that by 1980 available lead, zinc and tin will practically be used up. However, new ore discoveries are constantly increasing known reserves and the situation is unlikely to be as serious as the figures suggest. Technology advances rapidly and new sources of raw materials and new methods of obtaining them from diverse substances become known, while new metals and synthetic materials increasingly substitute for traditional and more expensive metals.

Nevertheless, we must envisage demands upon what in the long

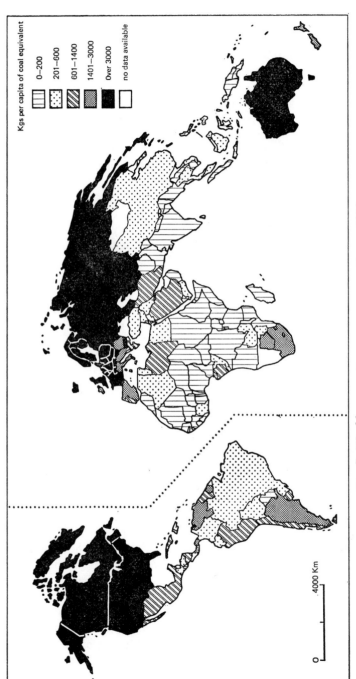

Fig. 7. World per capita energy consumption c. 1970.

Kgs per capita of coal equivalent

0–200
201–600
601–1400
1401–3000
Over 3000
no data available

4000 Km

run are limited, non-renewable resources. New discoveries in more remote areas may be made, leaner ores worked, but all will be reflected in an upward spiral of costs. Europe and the United States of America have built up their industrial civilizations while materials of all kinds have been readily available. The wealth they have accumulated suggests that even in the future their raw material needs can be met, but cost to the poorer developing countries will be forced up. These countries' requirements are likely to increase perhaps two or three times during the next twenty years, but the succeeding twenty years will see a massive increase with rising momentum.

RESOURCE PROBLEMS: ENERGY

The industrial revolution that has affected only a small part of the world, but has transformed world economy, led to the consumption during the last century of half as much energy as was used during the previous eighteen and a half centuries. This suggests that in grasping the fruits of modern technology the developing peoples must increasingly equip themselves with power. We must expect the rapid growth of world energy consumption to continue and although the rate of increase of demand from developed countries may slacken, rising demand from newly industrializing lands may well cause total consumption to double every twenty to twenty-five years. Industrialization depends upon the assured supplies of energy at competitive cost and the provision of this energy in its character and amount help to decide the nature and scope of industrial undertakings.

Problems arising from the enormously increased demand for energy when a substantial measure of development has been attained by under-developed countries have been eased during the last decade by the successful introduction of nuclear power for the generation of electricity. That consumption of energy increases markedly as levels of living rise may be appreciated from Table 8 where it will be seen that the majority of under-developed countries use less than 300 kg (6 cwt) of coal-equivalent per head, whereas Britain uses 5 tons and the United States 11 tons per head. The potential demand for energy during the next forty years is vast; the developed world is passing into a second industrial revolution involving petro-chemicals, synthetics, nuclear energy and automation, while the developing world is beginning in some ways to undergo the first stages that Britain passed through in the early nineteenth century.

Table 8: *Per capita energy consumption for selected countries, 1971*
(*kilogrammes, coal-equivalent*)

United States	11 240	Egypt	282
Canada	9330	Ghana	192
Sweden	6090	India	186
United Kingdom	5500	Kenya	171
Switzerland	3575	Sri Lanka	163
Japan	3270	Senegal	129
Venezuela	2520	Pakistan	96
Chile	1520	Uganda	72
Mexico	1270	Burma	68
Brazil	500	Ethiopia	32

SOURCE: *United Nations Statistical Yearbook, 1972*, table 140.

COAL, OIL AND WATER POWER

During the last two decades world coal consumption has been expanded faster than ever before, mainly due to industrial development in the USSR, China and India where coal is available as a major source of energy. On a global scale coal reserves are plentiful, although much is known to be in relatively inaccessible areas remote from population and industry and therefore costly to extract and market. Some two-thirds of world reserves lie in North America; relatively the eastern hemisphere is poorly endowed. A shortage of certain kinds of coal (e.g. for metallurgical coking) may become apparent and some industrial countries may find their supplies becoming scarce, for coal in its original bulky form is uneconomic to transport any distance overland. Certainly by the end of the century some acceleration in the demand for coal may be expected as new metallurgical and by-product chemical plants increase in number and as coal may begin to supplement crude oil as a source of liquid fuels.

Supplies of oil and natural gas, far more convenient and more easily transportable fuels than coal, are expected to be ample until the end of this century but thereafter to become scarcer and possibly to be supplemented by liquid fuel from oil shale and coal. Oil is likely to be of major importance to the developing countries in that its distribution is more generous to them than that of coal (Latin America and the Middle East hold 75 per cent of current known reserves), it can be transported much more easily, and like coal it has a raw material as well as a fuel and power value.

Coal, oil and natural gas are fossil fuels, part of the earth's store of capital and, in our life span, non-renewable. It is because of this fact that hydro-electric developments appear particularly attractive, for here the basic energy appears to be free and perpetual. What is frequently under-estimated is the enormous capital cost of creating vast hydro-electrical power stations and the great reservoirs usually necessary to smooth the normal variations of a river's discharge. Further, there is the high cost of transmitting the power to the consumer over any great distance (a much less important factor in thermal-electric costs for those power stations are usually established at the market). Hydro-electricity accounts for only about 6 per cent of the world's total energy consumption, although it represents nearly two-fifths of electrical energy generated. Topography and climate are the principal factors limiting the number and size of stations but there is still a great potential yet to be realized in the world. Unfortunately its distribution is very uneven, much of it being remote from industrial and populated centres and transmission of current over great distances is far too costly. Nevertheless, possession of conditions favouring hydro-electric power development is an important industrial asset, although often acting as a supplement to the other forms and, by its relative cheapness *at the site*, attracting to it, almost irrespective of the location, certain chemical and metallurgical industries requiring vast amounts of power for relatively inexpensive end products, such as nitrogenous fertilizers, aluminium and pulp manufacture.

It is rare for any country to lack a power potential in at least one of the foregoing fields. The real problem in the cases of developing countries has often been one of imperfect geological survey and unsatisfactory location, involving prohibitive cost of extraction and utilization. Since the end of the Second World War many new oil and natural gas discoveries have been made among developing countries, notably in Nigeria, Brazil, Pakistan, Libya and the Algerian Sahara. Frequently these discoveries are the fruits of many years' exploration and the expenditure of millions of pounds. The Nigerian discoveries came after twenty-one years of effort and exploration expenditure of £27 million by Shell-BP. The wells are very deep (including the deepest oil well in Africa at 14 558 feet) and many of them are situated in mangrove swamps, facts that have helped to make Nigerian oil so expensive to produce – one estimate puts the cost at eighty times that of Middle East oil.

NUCLEAR POWER

The advent of nuclear power offers great promise to many developing countries hampered in their advance by the lack, or high cost,
of their energy resources. We are still at the nursery stage in the
harnessing of nuclear power and efficiency of utilization is as yet
very low, but is improving rapidly as experience is gained. Because
of these continual improvements it is impossible to survey perform-
ance precisely, but in Britain in the reactors that came into use
during the early 1960s each ton of uranium fuel did the work of
nearly 20000 tons of coal. In Britain's early nuclear stations only
0·35 per cent of the uranium was burnt; at the 1 per cent rate of
utilization which seems attainable in the near future one ton of
uranium will equal 30000 tons of coal. The theoretical limit of
utilization is about 30 per cent, when one ton of uranium will do
the work of one million tons of coal. The uranium fuel in a reactor
lasts for several years and, being small in bulk and weight by comparison with coal and oil, can be transported easily about the world.
No shortage of the raw materials for nuclear power seems likely for
many centuries.

All this may seem most encouraging for developing countries but
a number of limitations must be examined. These power plants have
a far higher capital cost than conventional thermal power stations
(in Britain in 1974 about £230 per installed kilowatt against £55 per
kilowatt from conventional stations) but a lower fuel cost. It follows
that it is important to put the plant to maximum use and so secure
the lowest cost per unit of output. Such a plant would work at full
stretch to take the base load and might have a load factor, after
allowing for maintenance, of about 80 per cent. If the reactor is not
put to maximum use the cost of the power generated rises rapidly.
Developing countries examining possibilities of nuclear power must
take into account rates of interest they must pay on the very high
capital cost, they must consider the load factor the station can
operate to (whether there will be a market for the continuously high
output) and weigh up the costs of coal and/or oil procurement for
cheaper conventional power stations. The thermal efficiency of
these conventional power stations is also being improved, although
less rapidly than rising efficiency in nuclear power stations.

With such a number of variables it is impossible to quote average
costs per unit of power. In Britain electricity from nuclear power
stations is dearer than that from conventional stations and is likely

to remain so for at least another decade. However, these estimates apply to developed lands where established alternative resources compete fiercely. In many developing countries costs of these alternative sources of energy may be higher and their cost advantage over nuclear power much less.

So far nuclear power stations have been constructed in most of the advanced countries, but already it is possible to buy complete nuclear power plants from these countries including the erection and putting into working order, and with a guaranteed supply of uranium fuel. Japan, India and Brazil have already availed themselves of this new service. It is still too early to determine how far the majority of developing countries are likely to benefit by these energy advances; it is worth remembering, however, that in the long run the fact that fossil fuels provide not merely energy but industrial raw materials may be more decisive to prospects and future industrial status.

HUMAN RESOURCES

In this brief survey and appraisal of resources discussion of human resources, perhaps the most important, has been left to the end. There is now a growing awareness of the paramount place man himself holds in the process of economic development. In the long run success or failure must depend upon the capacity and adaptability of the people in adopting new techniques and new ways of life, in the will to work and to make sacrifices, in their understanding and discipline as traditional ways are superseded and new social orders and conditions arise. These are enormous demands upon what are all too often communities of illiterate peasants. To train and transform such human resources presents the greatest of problems to newly developing countries and requires much time. The industrial and technological fruits of one or more centuries' growth in developed lands may now be imported and grasped almost immediately by developing countries. Capital may be attracted, skill and 'know-how', in limited quantities, hired or borrowed, but clearly in themselves these things alone do not spell development unless the participation of the mass of the people is included in the forward movement.

Broadly we may discern three kinds of personnel necessary in commercial undertakings; the largest component being the workers and operatives themselves, then the smaller clerical, administrative and executive group, and finally the far smaller body of entrepreneurs, those who are prepared to accept risks and to initiate and translate projects from paper to actuality. Under-developed lands by definition have practically no force of industrially skilled labour available for new development projects. The mass of their peoples are untutored peasants frequently still in loose feudal relationships with the large landowners, conservative in their outlook, their ways moulded by tradition and the rhythm of the agricultural seasons. The absorption of these people into totally different and alien work and ways of life inevitably presents enormous problems and is often attended by unrest and unease at far-reaching social changes. The experiences of African workers in the developing industrial society of the town of Jinja in Uganda have been described as follows:

The African . . . has to carry out operations which are unfamiliar, on new materials and with new implements, in an unaccustomed environment in which timing and attention to detail have a previously undreamed of importance. He is expected to work for long stretches every day, at a time and place determined by others, to keep working all the time, and to associate during the working day with Europeans, Asians and Africans of other tribes whose behaviour bewilders and often antagonises him. He comes to regard his European and Asian superior as impatient, over-critical and unjust. They are in an incomprehensible hurry to complete every task.[8]

The training and building up of an efficient and reliable industrial labour force will be costly both in time and money. One of the greatest hindrances is the high degree of illiteracy: for example, 86 per cent of the Pakistani and 65 per cent of the Iranian population is illiterate. These populations, however, often prove very adaptable and frequently are surprisingly quick at mastering mechanical operations. The lack of experience of industrial occupation is often demonstrated in a resistance to the tempo of factory work, the regular hours and stereotyped regime, by high rates of absenteeism and a large labour turnover. This problem is least in cities where there may be acute competition for work, but is very real in smaller towns and country districts where new industries may well be located. It is also real in under-populated countries where the urge is rather to earn enough for particular targets – taxes, bride price for example – and then return to the farm. This is both costly and discouraging to the diversity of training and apprenticeship schemes on which industrial development leans. Farming routines and factory routines are very different and an efficient labour force for the one is likely to prove far less efficient in the other. A mixture of the two seems

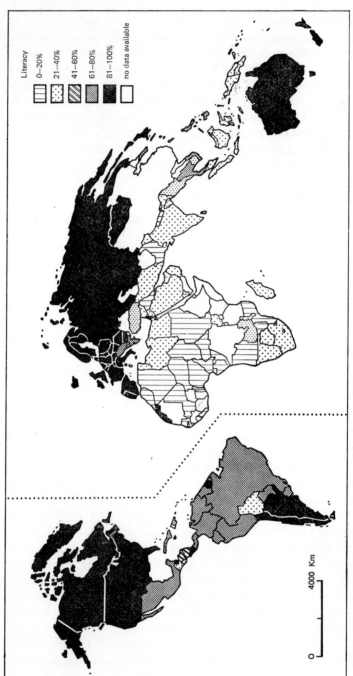

Legend:

Literacy
- 0–20%
- 21–40%
- 41–60%
- 61–80%
- 81–100%
- no data available

0   4000 Km

Fig. 8. World levels of literacy c. 1970.

incompatible: the industrial labour force must be divorced from the land, a requirement undoubtedly aided by the concomitant growth of urbanism bringing in its wake social and psychological changes.

It must be recognized that the great populations of so many of the developing countries while in a negative sense a drag upon capital formation also have positive value, for the abundant labour is a major resource provided that it can be trained and used effectively. Much expenditure is necessary to create the varied facilities for training, but much of this training of the rank and file, especially in light consumer goods industries, will be in the factories themselves. This suggests a considerable period of high-cost production for, as Lewis points out:

> If a factory is opened to weave cotton cloth, the management has to begin by training the workers in this operation. This training takes up to six months, before they are proficient; worse still, they can be trained only by using up yarn in the process of weaving, and the material wasted in this way is a heavy item of expense – even more so than their wages. This cost does not arise if a new factory is opened in an already established centre, since the management can hire its workers already trained.[9]

In many newly industrializing countries these costs may be particularly high since there may be no more than one or two factories in each particular trade and with absenteeism and a large labour turnover the creation of a pool of trained labour may be much prolonged. Considerations such as this should bring some qualification to the term 'cheap', applied almost universally to the labour force of developing countries. Wages may well appear cheap in comparison with those paid in developed countries, but the efficiency and productivity of the labour are generally far less for an appreciable time. In the mid 1950s the Egyptian textile industry, then well established, required sixteen operators per thousand spindles compared with five and four operatives per thousand spindles in Britain and the United States of America. Nevertheless simple operations controlling a machine such as that stamping out metal buttons reveal outputs as high as in Britain and the United States. The danger may well be that plentiful and apparently cheap labour may be used wastefully, but the real answer here is that to be competitive and flourish manufacturing industry must strive for ever greater efficiency. Japan and Hong Kong have shown the capability of Asians for highly skilled and highly efficient industrial production while maintaining low levels of labour costs.

Success in business hinges upon the smooth organization of a host of component parts, both human and material. In developed countries entrepreneurs can rely upon a considerable body of managerial ability, but in under-developed countries opportunities for acquiring such experience are rare and there is a dearth of competent men who possess both the necessary technical and commercial knowledge and the ability to organize labour and maintain efficient production. There are also acute shortages of such very necessary personnel as clerks and accountants, a reflection of the high levels of illiteracy. This lack of managerial talent coupled with administrative and clerical scarcity and shortage of capital has had the effect of furthering small-scale production in which such limitations press less severely.[10] Much depends upon census definitions of 'industrial establishments' which vary considerably, but we find that in 1939 some 74 per cent of Argentina's industrial establishments each employed no more than five workers, and the average number of employees in all establishments in 1944 was only sixteen; in Colombia in 1942 it was only eight and in Egypt in 1964 it was only three. China's recent emphasis upon the value and high place of small-scale enterprises is a notable example of making a virtue out of necessity.

Such small enterprises are of workshop rather than factory character which suggests a lack of modern low-cost methods of production and distribution, for economies of scale are lacking and the operations are labour-intensive rather than capital-intensive. Industrial progress in developing countries is characterized by the growth of such plants; they play an important part in the economy but, as will be discussed later, cannot in themselves constitute the full industrialization that is required.

In developed countries a distinctive feature of growth has been entrepreneurship: the emergence of a relatively small body of persons quick to discern opportunities and willing to promote and advance industrial undertakings despite the attendant risks. Under-developed countries lack such people since they can provide no nursery of the highly organized business society of the developed world. The need for such a body of experienced entrepreneurs is all-important to these countries if a wide front of industry and manufacturing is to be created and a responsible middle class is to develop. The alternative is a passive acceptance of government measures and the lack of flexibility and individuality: an open door to bureaucracy. Knowledge and experience wedded to initiative are the basic deficiencies today in developing lands, rather than a dearth of capital which has received overmuch attention from economists. As we have seen, deficiencies of capital can be much more readily supplied from external sources, but knowledge and experience can be lent only in more limited quantities and indigenous supplies will take years to develop.

The use of foreign knowledge as well as foreign capital is a characteristic of the spread of industrialization; this has applied in the past to the developed countries just as much as nowadays to those newly developing. With the desire for speedy industrial development and because of the increasingly complex make-up of modern industry this need for foreign advisers, technologists, managers, as well as capital, is expanding to huge proportions. Neither foreign capital nor the foreigners themselves are especially welcome in most countries, particularly in many of the newly independent states. Both are costly to borrow and both may constitute sources of friction as time passes. The real measure of help of the foreign expert is not only that he builds and operates industrial establishments, but that at the same time he trains local skill and stimulates local enterprise to take over and continue his tasks. Governments can do a great deal to further or delay development by their attitude to and treatment of foreigners and foreign investment. Foreigners and their money are urgently needed in developing lands; they are likely to become increasingly scarce commodities.

By now it should be quite clear that it takes far more than industry to industrialize. The foregoing discussion has served to outline the extreme complexity of factors concerning development in developing countries. The idea that such development primarily involves only economic and political factors is patently false. Development both demands and produces far-reaching changes in societies and the fabric of social life; it reacts both with and upon demographic factors; the whole operation is affected by and in turn leaves its impress upon the physical environment. The period of what might be regarded as spontaneous economic growth and adjustment to environmental conditions is past. The uneven pattern of such development, of rich and poor nations, the potency of demographic factors, the growth of world conscience, all have combined to create an era of economic planning. Time is short and the tasks gigantic, involving the mobilization and harmonizing of both national and international resources. Whether we have yet reached the stage of being able confidently to control and guide economic processes, and in so doing to adjust and mould societies and their vital processes, is uncertain. But immense social and economic experiments are now being made, for in no other way could there be much hope of success within short periods.

BIBLIOGRAPHICAL REFERENCES

1. E. Huntington, *Climate and Civilisation* (New Haven, 1924).
2. S. F. Markham, *Climate and the Energy of Nations* (Oxford, 1942), p. 32.
3. D. H. K. Lee, *Climate and Economic Development in the Tropics* (New York, 1957), p. 100.
4. N. C. Chaudhuri, *A Passage to England* (London, 1959), pp. 26–7.
5. F. B. Wells, 'Transport in the Rhodesian Copper Belt', *Geography* (1957), pp. 93–5.
6. B. Harris, 'Urbanisation Policy in India', *Proc. of the Regional Science Assoc.* (1959), p. 187.
7. J. E. Orchard, 'Industrialization in Japan, China Mainland, and India', *Annals of the Assoc. of American Geographers* (1960), p. 211.
8. C. Sofer, 'Working Groups in a Plural Society', *Industrial and Labour Relations Review* (1954), p. 73 (quoted by P. T. Bauer and B. S. Yamey, op. cit., p. 69).
9. W. A. Lewis, *Aspects of Industrialization* (Cairo, 1953), p. 31.
10. A. B. Mountjoy, 'Problems of Industrialization: An Egyptian Example', *Indian Geog. Jnl. Souvenir Vol.* (1951), pp. 20–3.

B. W. Hodder, *Economic development in the Tropics* (London, 1968).
E. A. G. Robinson (Ed.), *Economic Consequences of the Size of Nations* (New York, 1960).
U.S. Dept. Agric., *Climate and Man* (Washington, 1941).
N. Ginsburg, 'Natural Resources and Economic Development', *Annals of the Association of American Geographers* (1957), pp. 197–212.

7 The form of industrialization

Industrial growth commences in order to supply a growing home demand and begins with simple processing of agricultural and mineral commodities formerly traded in their raw state. Such industries include milling, leather tanning, oilseed pressing, spinning and weaving, brewing and brick-making.

Generally the early processing of agricultural commodities by hand, and later by hand-worked machines, was to remove waste matter, or change the produce into a more edible form, or to one that could be moved or stored more easily. Gradually processing became more complicated and with the development of commerce and communications the handicraft stage began to give way to power-operated machinery. These changes became consolidated with the growth of a money economy and expanding demand which have led to the manufacture of consumer goods both for home and export and finally, in some countries, to industries producing capital equipment.

FACTORS INFLUENCING THE SELECTION OF INDUSTRIES

The nature and scope of various industries and the possibilities of their adoption in developing countries are influenced by limitations already mentioned: namely, lack of skilled labour, lack of capital, lack of market and scarcity of foreign exchange. These impose restraints upon the kind, size and scope of the industrial development, the methods used, and the order of priorities. The dearth of skilled labour is one very serious handicap, imposing limits not simply on types of industrial activity, but also upon methods of working and the kinds of machinery introduced. Machines requiring individual operations of a comparatively simple level of skill are far more suitable than fewer more complicated machines each capable of a complex series of operations. Not only the operating but also the maintenance of the latter type of machine would be beyond the competence of practically all the local skill. The highly skilled engineer is a product of long training and tradition and plays a vital part in a modern factory; it will be a very long time before developing countries have such personnel in large numbers.

Another limitation is capital: it is both scarce and expensive and must be used to best advantage. The amount of capital investment particular industries require varies enormously. For comparative purposes, it may be expressed in terms of capital required per worker, and in Britain this varies from about £620 in the china and earthenware industry to £13 350 in oil refining. In British West Africa the initial amounts of capital per worker recently needed to establish certain industries included £550 for a canning factory, £3000 for a vehicle assembly plant, and £13 150 for a cement works.[1] These high costs have to be borne in mind in selecting projects and it does not follow that those projects with highest yield per unit of invested capital are automatically the best. The returns of some projects, notably public utilities, are not to be measured solely in monetary terms, but by the fact that projects such as railways, port facilities and electricity supplies resemble catalysts, reacting upon other industries and making them far more remunerative. Further, some capital-intensive projects produce far greater output than many with a low ratio of capital to labour; thus selection in terms of low capital investment per worker in turn is not necessarily best.

The size of the market limits the division of labour and the inducement to invest and is therefore a further determinant of the character of industrial development. Here we are concerned not merely with numbers but with the size of the subsistence-only element in the economy, of the availability of export markets, and governmental policies regarding competing imports of manufactured goods. It is possible to satisfy the home demand for manufactures of many developing countries with surprisingly few modern industrial establishments and a smaller industrial labour force than is generally supposed. A single modern factory employing about fifty operatives could manufacture enough biscuits to satisfy the complete Ghanaian and Nigerian demand and, in Nigeria at present a single factory employing 150 workers supplies one-fifth of that country's needs. As we have seen, home demand for manufactures may be expanded if productivity in other sectors of the economy is increased, but where large-scale rural under-employment prevails industrial development needs to be on a very great scale to absorb surplus population, and is only likely to do this by finding export markets to supplement the limited home demand. Countries seeking success in export markets must extract the maximum benefit from low industrial wages, the one great advantage they usually possess. To obtain entry into established markets manufactured exports must be highly competitive in price and quality. Low industrial wages do not necessarily imply low labour costs, for this depends upon the productivity of the labour and the degree of skill. It has been estimated that wages in British West Africa are about one-tenth of those of the United Kingdom, while the difference in industrial productivity, given similar equipment, averages one-third to one-half. Where wages are low and skill and productivity high, as in the Hong Kong textile industry, marked success has attended the penetration of export markets.

Problems of foreign exchange also throw emphasis upon production for export, for even if much foreign capital is available as grants or loans, subsequently interest and capital repayments must be made. Foreign exchange shortage means a favouring of activities requiring a minimum of imported machinery and using indigenous rather than imported raw materials; in other words it favours some emphasis upon labour-intensive technology and small rather than large establishments. Such a pattern of development is also favoured where labour costs (based on low wages) are low, for in this kind of operation labour costs form a major element of total costs.

Theoretically, in examining the character of industrial development in developing lands, the classical doctrine of comparative advantage might seem to have substantial application, but in practice it may not be so, especially in initial phases. According to the theory, a country will gain by specializing in the production of those commodities in which its comparative advantage is greatest, exporting those goods in exchange for ones where its comparative cost advantage is less. The theory underlines optimum use of resources and invokes international levels of cost comparison. However, a substantial body of industry in developing countries cannot be assessed in this way, for its products really do not enter into world trade (e.g. much food processing, building, electricity generating, and other utilities). Also we must remember that the pattern of comparative costs is not static; if it were so there might be very little industrial development in under-developed lands and established advantages of the industrial nations would be omnipotent. The reason why governments are so intimately involved is that they alone have the power to interfere with the play of forces in the market and to alter comparative costs in the home market by supporting and sustaining new industries through their birth pangs and early years. A brief discussion of the role of governments in this connection follows later.

THE INFLUENCE OF TRANSPORT COSTS

The economic geographer is well aware that the interplay of certain factors such as value and bulk of raw materials in relation to the character of the end product, cost of assembly of raw materials and of distribution of the finished goods, amounts of fuel, power and labour required, all have a bearing upon the locations within a country of particular industrial plants. These factors also carry varying weight in determining the character of industry and the nature of the manufacturing that a newly industrializing country may successfully undertake. One of the most decisive among these factors is transport cost. Cost of transport makes local manufacture advantageous where heavy low-value raw materials are required and are available locally; also it is advantageous to set up local industry either on home or imported raw materials where the finished products are bulkier, and therefore more expensive to transport, than the raw materials. In these categories we may include cement, bricks and tiles, furniture and motor-vehicle assembly. Raw materials that vary little in bulk when manufactured are not much affected by transport costs nor are those materials of such high value that transport costs form a relatively small proportion of total costs. In these groups we may include cigarettes, clothing, cotton and other textile materials. Transport costs would be similar whether raw materials or finished goods were imported and the high value relative to amount of raw material, bulk and weight makes exports possible.

On the other hand transport costs discourage setting up local industry where raw materials have to be imported and lose weight in processing, for this would incur freight rates being paid on useless waste material (e.g. pulp and paper utilizing only two-fifths of the pulp wood, and iron and steel manufacture may be regarded as examples, but it should be remembered in the latter industry where more than one raw material is involved that a country may have some of the raw materials at sufficiently low procurement cost to offset freight rates on the import of the others). Also a country lacking good supplies of various fuels is discouraged from establishing those industries where fuel requirements are heavy owing to the high cost of transporting fuel.

This outline, in many respects oversimplified, should help to explain the general pattern of industrial growth in most developing countries, especially those not well endowed with fuel and ore supplies. A range of food-processing industries first becomes established, based upon local agricultural raw materials and proximity to market and freed from external competition by the perishability of the raw material – milk processing, baking, the canning and preserving of fruit and vegetables, and beverage manufacture such as aerated drinks and beer (where water is an important raw material). Then industries based upon wood, such as furniture-making, and those connected with construction and derived from local mineral resources: cement, pre-stressed concrete, bricks and tiles, sanitary ware, glass, pottery, crockery. Assembly industries follow, these being based upon cheaper transport costs of importing component parts assembled locally to make, e.g. bicycles, motor vehicles. These are the customary early industrial activities that arise, for their resource bases are either practically ubiquitous or, as we have seen, they are generally sheltered from competition by transport costs and perishability.

With these industries we find others appearing that have less substantial bases and sometimes more hazardous lives. These produce such consumer goods as textiles, clothing, footwear, soap, cigarettes. Unless there is the advantage of local raw materials these industries gain no advantage from the level of freight rates on raw materials against finished goods and are likely to be exposed to competition of mass-produced goods from abroad (often of higher and more reliable quality). The main off-setting advantage they have is low labour costs, but generally this is insufficient and these industries exist (and at times stagnate) beneath a protective tariff.

The industries listed above are the major ones established during the 'pre-take-off' period, generally restricted in character and scale by limited demand, capital, skill, and public utilities, etc. However, these articles, which in many cases can be based upon indigenous raw materials, are those that absorb an increasing proportion of spending power as incomes begin to rise above subsistence level, consequently there is a considerable potential home market for them in all underdeveloped lands. A disadvantage worth remembering, however, is that for these very reasons every developing country is able to make these goods for itself. In these goods there is little scope for export, for, as we have seen, earlier world trade in these commodities is scarcely expanding. For countries that possess resources of fuel and ores the industrial path is likely to be somewhat smoother. Metal manufactures form substantial proportions of the imports of developing countries and command expanding markets in developed lands, consequently world demand for metal goods is increasing and export markets are more readily available. Absence of ores, particularly iron ore, places a curb upon the character and degree of industrial expansion. If fuel is readily available and wages low some metal manufactures are possibly based upon imported ingots, but generally they are limited to such items as nails, nuts and bolts, pots and pans, and simple agricultural implements.

The need for export markets has been stressed as being a key factor in successful industrial development of over-populated developing countries, but the range of goods likely to be exported successfully is small, particularly so if ores and fuel are not plentiful. Transport costs now act in reverse and only favour goods made from indigenous raw materials that lose weight in manufacture. It is not feasible to use imported raw materials for export industries unless a great deal of labour and skill lavished upon them will materially raise their value (e.g. watches, instruments, high-quality ceramics), or where the ratio of value to weight is sufficiently high for cost of transport to be a minor element in the final cost (e.g. textile raw materials). Success in these activities depends especially upon low labour costs (generally present) allied with considerable skill and technical knowledge (generally absent); it follows that the training and education of the labour force needs to have a high place. Hong Kong provides an example of success here; her millions are supported by widely disseminated exports of cheap textiles, toys, electronic and transistor devices, etc.

INFRA-STRUCTURE NEEDS

Advances in the range of manufactures by means of successful new promotions and the expansion of existing industry from workshop to factory character will depend essentially upon prior or parallel expansion of utilities, education and technical training: the establishment of what is now called the infra-structure. The provision of railways, power stations, harbour installations, schools, hospitals, in themselves large employers of labour, also serves to stimulate local industry, especially the constructional ones such as cement manufacture, manufactures of pre-cast and reinforced concrete, bricks and tiles, metal windows, pipes and tubes.

The considerable capital investment and the lengthy period of fulfilment required in establishing the infra-structure is now an accepted part of planned or systematic development, and reflects changing views during the decade 1950–60 when economic planning with the enhanced role of government became internationally respectable. A widespread experience in many developing countries was of industries mushrooming during the war and immediate post-war years and failing because their costs were too high and quality too poor or, despite this, surviving at public expense thanks to government support. This has brought home the realization that industrialization cannot afford to develop on a patchy and haphazard trial and error basis with mis-directed and misused capital investment, but that first a proper infra-structure beneficial to all sectors of the economy is essential. Thus the closing years of the 1950s saw a variety of basic works being put into effect in a considerable number of the world's poorer countries. *Afghanistan's* first Five Year Plan (1956–61) concentrated on education, the provision of roads, basic irrigation works and power stations. At the end of the period four hydro-electric stations had been built and three others were under construction, while two cement factories were constructed and coal mining began. *Pakistan*, under its first Five Year Plan (1955–60), devoted 31 per cent of the capital expenditure to agriculture, water and power development; while *India* in her four completed Five Year Plans allotted to communications and power 40 per cent, 38 per cent, 33 per cent and 32 per cent of total allocations.

Among these basic works are iron and steel plants, not in themselves utilities, but nevertheless the foundation of a large sector of the industrial field. Modern civilization is based on iron and steel and the establishment of iron and steel works is one of the most desired features of planned development, opening the doors to a great range of other industries, particularly those making heavy capital goods. Not every country possesses raw materials, fuel bases and transport facilities for this industry which, owing to very considerable loss of weight on fabrication, cannot be operated economically on imported supplies. A number of post-war examples may be cited where these economic factors have been ignored and iron and steel works erected for prestige or strategic reasons. Hungary's iron and steel town of Sztalinvaros, on the Danube forty miles south of Budapest, is such an example. It is a relic of autarkic policies and up to 1960 the works had cost about £200 million and had an annual capacity of 600000 tons of pig iron and 350000 tons of crude steel.

Hungary has no iron ore deposits and the plant obtains its ore from Krivoi Rog in the USSR. Four-fifths of the coal is Hungarian, but of indifferent coking quality, and is combined with coking coal imported from Poland. The economic soundness of the project is doubtful, but under a Communist regime this is not made public.[2] A project likely to prove more sound is the iron and steel plant completed in 1969 at Annaba (Bône) in Algeria. This cost £126 million and has an output of 400000 tons of metal per annum. Here the country possesses the fuel and raw material supplies necessary for the industry; she is, in fact, a major exporter of high-quality iron ore. A developing country having the resources necessary for an iron and steel industry has much to gain from its establishment. A far wider range of manufactures becomes possible, costs to already established metal-using industries are lowered, foreign exchange will be saved and export possibilities created. It is unlikely that sufficient skill and management ability to run such works will be built up locally for a number of years, but even at very high salaries the hiring of foreign skill and knowledge (provided that these are passed on) is here a good investment. Great prospects for the future are opened up; as time passes and skills develop, engineering, the manufacture of machinery for factories and of other capital goods becomes possible, and also the development of chemical and fertilizer manufacturing industries based upon the by-products of the coking process, of particular value to agrarian countries.

Oil refineries also offer much scope for associated chemical and plastics industries, but these plants are very expensive and need highly skilled staff. There has been a swing away from the earlier location of many refineries at the oil field to sites nearer the larger markets for the refined products and by-products, as in Western Europe. It must be expected that full-scale refineries will not be established easily in developing countries, even if they themselves are crude-oil producers, until substantial home markets for their products arise, but basic refineries without cracking and by-product plants are now being built in a number of populous developing countries, including Gabon, Tanzania, Malaya and Costa Rica.

THE CHARACTER OF INDUSTRIAL DEVELOPMENT:
(1) LABOUR-INTENSIVE POLICIES

Power plants, iron and steel works and oil refineries require immense investments of capital; they in themselves give relatively little employment (i.e. the capital investment per worker is very high), but the output per worker is high and particularly beneficial to a very wide sector of the developing industrial economy. It is possible, however, that the return per unit of capital invested in such capital-intensive processes will be less initially than if the money had been invested in a greater number of other and more labour-intensive projects. Decisions as to the appropriate capital intensity in the industrialization of a developing country are of fundamental importance, since they will have notable effects upon the character and pattern of the industrial development. They will require early examination of the emphasis to be given to 'heavy' as opposed to 'light' industry and thus the tempo of industrialization itself, for many experts consider there is an implicit correlation between capital per worker and the type of industrial output. In other words, there are not only capital- and labour-intensive *processes* but also capital- and labour-intensive *industries*. Labour-intensive production is assumed to be of small or medium scale of operation and to make 'light' consumer goods, while capital-intensive production is identified with large-scale industrial production of 'heavy' or capital goods. It is sufficient here to remark that these are general concepts; the mutual relationships lack statistical proof, mainly because such data are scarce.

In many developing lands there is no shortage of labour, but the amount of capital likely to be available is limited. This is generally the reverse of conditions pertaining in the developed countries, where labour is scarce and capital more abundant. Industry there has become more and more capital-intensive; machines replace scarce labour, technology is introduced and an outlook quite unsuited to conditions in developing countries has developed. Here, then, we find considerable differences; it is clear that particular technologies in use in developed countries need not be taken over wholesale by developing countries, and in many cases they may be inappropriate. Where labour is plentiful it is extravagant to use capital as a substitute, although there is a case for it if machines can replace a dearth of skill (e.g. in textile, boot and shoe industries).

There is a strong body of opinion that where capital is limited it is better to spread it thinly in order to cover a greater labour force, in other words to place emphasis upon labour-intensive industries and methods. Here low labour costs can exert their maximum effects on total costs. By these means there is more development and a wider distribution of purchasing power among

E

those who will quickly spend it, mainly (it is hoped) on consumer goods. Much of the labour used might otherwise be unproductive, and capital saved by the use of this labour can be used for the production of other goods and the employment of yet more labour. As a result total production and income will be greater than if more highly mechanized methods had been used. These views favour small-scale undertakings, between the cottage handicraft unit and the large-scale factory in both size and techniques. Other advantages claimed are that the volume of production from such plants is more likely to accord with the restricted market for the products (a few days' production of a large modern shoe factory would serve to satisfy the present effective annual demand for shoes in a country such as Morocco). Also small-scale industries making use of electric power are less exacting in locational demands and can be widely distributed and thus help to avoid excessive agglomerations of people in large urban areas, necessitating high cost of housing, utilities and sanitation. There is also the view that establishing small-scale industries is a natural first step whereby skill, technique and markets may be developed for subsequent large-scale operations. These policies are supported by Dr Schumacher under the title 'intermediate technology' and a charitable trust has been set up in Britain to gather information on low-cost technologies and on self-help techniques. Intermediate technology comes between primitive traditional methods and the costly sophisticated technologies of the advanced countries; it seeks to devise technologies where the capital cost of a workplace may be no more than about £100 and where simple techniques and local raw materials are employed. Dr Schumacher also cites an important social aspect, that the development of workplaces where people live and not merely in metropolitan areas will help arrest the flood of unemployed to the towns.[3] These views, of course, do not rigidly bar large-scale industry, but put most emphasis upon medium and small-scale ones, believing that they give more employment per unit of invested capital. A real danger is that little of the surplus product is likely to be saved for reinvestment and industrial expansion will be slow.

(2) CAPITAL-INTENSIVE POLICIES

The opposite case is also a strong one, and is based on the premise that a cumulative increase in production and national income stems from ever-increasing productivity of labour. This increasing productivity can only come about through the adoption of increasingly efficient techniques and appliances, requiring heavy application of capital. Far higher productivity per worker is possible with capital-intensive processes (although a smaller return per unit of capital than with labour-intensive ones) and, if the profits per worker are continually reinvested, the net product will grow at a faster rate than that of the less intensive ones. This means, in fact, that while employment will be lower in the early years it accelerates rapidly and soon outstrips the initially higher levels obtaining in labour-intensive industries.

Investment should take as its aim the raising of productive capacity rather than the provision of the greatest number of jobs; with the attainment of one the other will follow. Higher productivity begets higher surpluses, allowing yet more capital for investment; thus an upward spiral may be envisaged. To this end emphasis on the establishment of capital goods industries rather than consumer goods industries is a further logical step, and some experts favour massive capital-intensive investment in basic industries producing equipment goods which later make possible a more rapid increase of consumer goods. Labour-intensive production lacks this self-accelerating character and with it an economy is likely to stagnate. Early Egyptian industrial development between the wars demonstrates this feature, while modern Indian planned development leans much more upon capital-intensive methods.

It is clear that both policies are vulnerable at some points and also that in any actual country (as opposed to theoretical models for planning purposes) the real decision concerns the proportion of the limited resources to be employed one way and the other. It is here that economic arguments may become subordinated to social and political policies. Thus we find the following industrial activities recommended by a mission to a heavily populated Asian country, their view clearly favouring labour-intensive industrialization: rice milling, coir fibre manufacture, cotton textiles by small-scale production ('The mission recognises that a fairly large and vertically integrated spinning and weaving mill would produce cloth more cheaply . . . nevertheless other economic as well as social reasons make it imperative to encourage the development . . . of small-scale production'), manufacture of footwear, metal-working industries including hardware, brass and aluminium products, ceramics, agricultural implements, building materials, galvanizing and electro-plating.[4]

The influence of a social policy designed to avoid the creation of an industrial proletariat undoubtedly influenced the recommendations of other experts to a Middle East country. They urged the establishment of an integrated complex of small-scale and handicraft activities, and recommended that spinning, dyeing and finishing of cotton be carried out by factory techniques and that sizing, weaving and knitting be done by handicraft, cottage industrial methods. To avoid the social effects of big agglomerations of industrial working population they suggested the building of three or four small textile units in villages some 15–20 km apart. With modern communications it was contended that they could be run as one big factory by one management and one technical service.[5]

Another expert to a different Asian country recommended capital-intensive industrialization with particular emphasis upon large-scale capital goods and heavy machinery industries, and cited the country's economic position as justification. There was a satisfactory foreign trade position and no balance of payments difficulties, a high level of food production and a large reserve of man-power allowing development of basic industries without reducing production in other sectors. He rejected proposals for the expansion of cottage industries on the score that it merely disguised unemployment by means of social relief since differences in the efficiency of production would involve subsidies to the cottage industries and output quotas on competing products of large-scale industries.[6]

Efficiency or output per worker cannot be taken entirely as a reflection of capital investment or size of plant although a general correlation is discernible. Professor Mukerjee, for instance, has shown that from 1946 to 1949 there was an increase in capital intensity in a number of India's manufacturing industries, in most cases accompanied by a rise in output per worker.[7] Studies to discover optimum techniques (capital- or labour-intensive) in various industries are only slowly being carried out, but it is clear that in some there may be room for combinations of methods. Further, it is not always necessary to introduce the latest European or American machinery or equipment, often very complicated and designed for very different settings where labour costs are very high. It may be uneconomic to take the newest machines, simple models – even second-hand – may give a better return.

Industrial advisers to developing countries are concerned with overcoming the technical problems involved in raising productivity in industrial plants, and it has been remarked that a general pattern emerging from their recommendations shows a ready resort to mechanization. To technicians from industrialized countries faced with the task of improving volume, quality and uniformity of output and in reducing unit costs this recommendation is in keeping with their experience. They are far less concerned with the social problems surrounding unemployment. However, as a rule modifications are possible and, while techniques may be up-to-date, the size, degree of capitalization and specialization in a wide range of industries will not for some time match those in developed countries. Some heavy industries however must be accepted with very little change: iron and steel works, chemical industries producing sulphuric acid, caustic soda, nitrogenous fertilizer need much capital and cannot be operated economically on a small scale.

PLANNING STRATEGY

As a preliminary to planning for industrialization the adoption of a broad strategic framework is a necessary first step. Those favouring balanced development, and with Rostow's economic history as guide, point out the dependence of industry upon agriculture: the pace of development in the one depends upon the pace of advance in the other. In less-developed countries agriculture is the principal source of employment, of capital and of foreign exchange. It provides the internal purchasing power that creates the home market for manufactures, and its food surpluses determine the number of workers that can be sustained outside agriculture. Thus, logically but paradoxically, in the early stages of an industrialization programme resources should be concentrated upon the development of agriculture.

This 'agriculture first' model is stoutly opposed by an 'industry first' school. Their view is that agriculture will not become more productive unless it can be stimulated by expanding markets and better prices. Many farmers produce no more than what is needful for subsistence, but if tempted by cheap manufactured goods they would produce more to earn enough to buy them. The early establishment of industry would create these conditions, spurring on the expansion of food and raw material production and siphoning off labour from the land. Output per head would be raised and foreign exchange would be saved.

That these are deceptively simple arguments become clear if real-life conditions are examined. Rostow's examples relate mainly to the nineteenth century, when industry was less sophisticated and cost per workplace was moderate. Also populations are far heavier today and pressure upon the land limits its response as a source of investment capital, which would be far below the huge sums needed. Further progress would depend upon the efficient development of capital-intensive industry with export markets, for with prevailing heavy rates of population increase the expansion of the home market would be limited and the whole project hazardous. Clearly choices between alternatives, or a judicious blending of them, provide the development planners with their most difficult task.

THE ROLE OF GOVERNMENTS

This discussion has been designed to demonstrate the variety of conflicting interests involved in determining development targets, and the choice of means to achieve them. Social, economic, technical and strategic factors must be evaluated and governments must decide upon the tempo of development by means of their power of controls and emphasis upon long-term or short-term measures. To mobilize and employ all the forces available in the struggle for development requires that each government of developing countries prepares and puts into effect a general economic plan. The heart of such a plan is to procure the necessary capital in order to raise the amount of investment and so to increase productivity, utilizing both internal and external sources. Given the capital, the plan should allocate proportions of it to the various sectors of the economy: transport, communications, power production, manufacturing industry, both 'heavy' and 'light', agriculture, health and education. In turn, detailed proposals for these should be made.

Problems affecting the formation of capital have been discussed in Chapter 5. No developing country can hope to raise anything like the total capital it needs entirely from external sources; increasing quantities must come from investments and savings of its own population, and governmental policies become shaped to encourage and often to enforce this. The discipline of a developing population becomes most tried after the first fruits of development gradually appear. Expanding incomes lead to an increasing demand for consumer goods, and government measures designed to encourage saving and reinvestment attempt to damp down this demand in order to keep control over the development process. There is the further advantage that keeping demand for consumer goods in check allows for more investment and for the growth of the more expensive capital goods industries. Some of the enhanced demand will be for imported goods, and this has the added disadvantage of affecting the foreign exchange position. Consequently developing countries invariably impose import restrictions in one form or another, and these have the further effect of working to protect home manufactures.

Policies of protection are frequently criticized, yet if a developing country is ruthlessly determined to dedicate its powers to development such a policy becomes necessary. While the aim that new industries should pay their way is laudable, it should also be clear that these standards have less immediate application in underdeveloped lands where investments are being made that for a long period may be unprofitable, yet are necessary to create external economies for subsequent industries. Much early investment in manufacturing industry is on a similar basis: it would not take place if some protection or inducement were not afforded, for the disincentives to manufacturing at that stage are too great, this being the reason why the investments were not made earlier.

New industries in developing countries take some time to become going concerns; they must train their labour, which will affect both quality and quantity of production; they may have to pay high rates for services and power; with few other industries operating there will be few external economies; they may find difficulty in breaking into the market, probably supplied by imported goods, and may work below capacity for a considerable period. Not surprisingly, costs of production are likely to be high during this initial period and these industries are in a competitively weak position. All these difficulties should lessen as development proceeds and, provided there is a reasonable chance that the industry will duly pay its way, there is a good case for protection or some form of government help.

The main justification, however, is that the very existence of these young industries is giving a substantial return to the developing state beyond the mere value of their production. It is generally true that every new enterprise improves the external economies of other concerns. The more factories there are, the cheaper can be the supply of gas, electricity, oil fuel, repair facilities, and the greater the expansion of the industrial labour force. Concentration as opposed to dispersion of industry particularly permits further mutual advantages in the use of raw materials, by-products, transport and other services so that a cumulative reduction of cost may be envisaged as development proceeds. Certainly dispersion of industry might moderate the growth of metropolitan centres and reduce the heavy social costs attendant upon large urban areas, and it might also reduce the impact of the growing dualism in the economy, but it is rarely favoured on economic grounds.

The system of protection deserves criticism if it is given in an unplanned economy to haphazard industrial promotions that never become competitive, for the higher prices are a burden on the consumer and contract rather than expand the market. The further effect is that the rural population is financing industrialization, for protection raises the price of manufactures relative to agricultural products. To some degree this may be necessary and must be accepted, but the danger is that inequality between rural and urban incomes grows and a severe drift from the land into urban unemployment takes place.

The range of government help and methods that can be employed are very great. Frequently tariffs are levied on selected categories of imported goods, roughly in the form nil on machinery, low on raw materials, moderate on semi-finished goods and heavy on finished manufactures. Internal freight rates to and from ports and factories also may be adjusted on similar lines, with especially favourable rates for moving indigenous raw materials. Other forms of help may be as loans at low interest rates; subsidies especially to goods seeking export markets; exemptions from certain taxes for a stated period and, in some countries, preferential treatment by government order departments.

All this indicates that many of the young industries depend for their profits largely upon government interventions. An unfortunate but natural response is to lobby and bring pressure to bear on the government for further support, rather than to seek greater efficiency of operation and the cutting of costs.

PREPARING THE PLAN

The drafting of a plan for economic development follows the basic decisions on social and economic aims. These would be expressed in terms of permitted annual percentage increase in consumption, the degree of unemployment to be tolerated, the amount of foreign exchange deficit to be allowed. A United Nations publication has described the procedure as follows:

The basic principles having been formulated are expressed mathematically by a system of equations, the next step – the operational part of planning – would consist in aggregating the relevant economic and technical information in a programming matrix; the system would then be 'solved' for those variables which it is sought to evaluate. In fact the whole process begins by drawing up as large a list as possible of economic projects both existing and proposed, the inclusion of an activity involving no commitment whatever as to its retention in the final plan or its numerical importance. The list should contain not only such conspicuous and much talked about labour-saving and capital-intensive projects as modern steel production, aluminium production, heavy fertiliser production, etc., but also a number of labour-intensive activities . . . such as road building, slum clearing, minor irrigation, handloom weaving, etc. Only by including a sufficiently large spectrum of such activities will it be possible at a later stage to find optimum solutions that can really satisfy the desired conditions of employment in the transition period. Each listed activity will be described by economists and engineers, who will tabulate current operations and capital requirements for both existing and proposed enterprises. Information concerning current operations, that is, activities resulting in a more or less continuous flow of goods and services, will relate to input – wages, salaries, ownership income, taxes, purchases from other enterprises, imports and such items – and output of given products or groups of similar products ('product-mix') for any given period; the input and output data will also cover the physical quantities involved. Information concerning capital investment will relate to size, required construction period, type of ownership, etc. The information, together with data relating to the supply of domestic and foreign capital, will then be aggregated in a programming matrix; the mathematical solution of the system, obtained by a method based on linear programming, will provide the answer to such questions as the optimum combination of industries, the respective levels of investment in, and rate of growth of, producer and consumer goods industries, the maximum rate of expansion, etc., corresponding to the stated goals.[8]

BIBLIOGRAPHICAL REFERENCES

1. United Africa Co., *Statistical and Economic Review*, No. 23 (1959), p. 6.

2. *The Times* (14 March 1960).

3. E. F. Schumacher, *Rural Industries*, in M. W. Clark, *India at Midpassage*, ODI (London, 1964), pp. 30–9.

4. United Nations, *Industrialization and Productivity*, Bulletin 1 (New York, 1958), p. 13.

5. Ibid., p. 14.

6. Ibid., p. 15.

7. K. Mukerjee, 'Employment and substitution of Capital for Labour', *Indian Economic Jnl.* (1956), p. 105.

8. United Nations, op. cit., p. 12.

E. M. Hoover, *The Location of Economic Activity* (New York, 1948).

R. C. Estall and R. O. Buchanan, *Industrial Activity and Economic Geography* (London, 1966) (especially Chapter 2).

J. Tinbergen, *Development planning* (London, 1967).

8 The progress of industrialization
I. Ghana and Nigeria; Chile; Hong Kong

Every nation runs an individual course in the cross-country development race; each faces and must overcome a series of obstacles and difficulties, some of them being individual to its own course. It seems appropriate, therefore, to scrutinize certain aspects of industrial development in a few selected countries in order to demonstrate from actual examples the character of the problems to be faced, and the varying progress being made. Full treatment is impossible here: instead a variety of facets have been selected to exemplify aspects of the body of theory previously advanced with, finally, an examination in some detail of one country's progress in industrialization.

GHANA AND NIGERIA

West Africa provides us with a region where environmental difficulties pose severe problems to economic development but where a number of newly independent African states are attempting to co-ordinate their resources and plan for their future. Ghana and Nigeria are examples of such countries. Both these independent countries exhibit social and economic conditions widely different from a number of other developing lands. Both have had early development plans disrupted by revolution and, in the case of Nigeria, by civil war. Another vital difference is that neither suffers from over-population and each has land still available for agricultural expansion. Low per capita incomes here result from chronic under-utilization of resources rather than substantial utilization with too many people sharing the returns. Early plans for developing industrial sectors were modest, then Ghana raised the pace in the early 1960s before the fall of President Nkrumah, and now Nigeria is speeding industrial projects with the oil boom of the early 1970s.

The rate of increase of Ghana's population (totalling 9 000 000 in 1973) has steepened during the last decade. It may now average as much as 3 per cent per annum and the population is therefore likely to have doubled well before the end of the century. The increasing weight of population is to be found in the prosperous southern part of the republic, where urban growth has been remarkable. Since 1938 the chief towns, Accra (the capital, pop. 600000), the Sekondi-Takoradi port area (160000) and Kumasi (350000), have multiplied their population eight or nine times. The south possesses all the railways and most of the road network; the north remains relatively inaccessible and undeveloped.

Ghana's wealth is derived mostly from the large African-owned and -operated cocoa-farming business. It was the cocoa-tax revenues that provided much of the development capital during the 1950s. The Cocoa Marketing Board between 1939 and 1958 is estimated to have accumulated £107 million net surplus. This sum gives some indication of the important part cocoa plays in the economy; in recent years cocoa exports have accounted for 64 per cent of export revenue. The vulnerability of Ghana to fluctuation in world demand and the seriousness of falling prices need little emphasis, and led to plans for diversification by promoting the expansion of the timber industry and of the industrial sector in her economy. In addition, growing food consumption has outstripped local food supply and an increasing volume of food is now imported (16 per cent of imports by value in 1969). Either local agriculture and industry must become more productive in order to reduce imports, or exports must be increased to pay for the growing food imports. The growth of import-saving local industries is therefore one of the goals of development.

In 1951 a first Development Plan was prepared involving a public investment of £102 million. The then Gold Coast government put most emphasis upon the building up of the less spectacular but essential public services – communications, education, water supplies, health – realizing that the existing infra-structure was quite inadequate to sustain substantial development. The following years saw £34 million devoted to communications and harbours, including a considerable programme of road construction, railway modernization, construction of power stations and harbour developments at Takoradi and the commencement of the building of another major port at Tema. The second Development Plan (1959–64) suspended in 1962 in favour of a Seven Year Plan (1964–71) was far more ambitious: it required £243 million investment, more than double that of the first plan and was to be completed in five years. The spending of a further £100 million on a major hydro-electric scheme on the River Volta was also proposed.

The allocation to commerce and industry in both Plans was small since it was hoped that with the development of a firm infra-structure private capital would be attracted to exploit industrial opportunities. The range of manufactures developing during the period of the first Plan followed the customary pattern and included brick and tile manufacture, beverage industries, food processing, biscuit and soap manufacture, pottery, nails and foundry products and the assembly of bicycles and refrigerators. The more ambitious second Plan led to a steel mill, a ship-repair yard, the introduction of textile industries, boot and shoe manufacture, cement milling, the manufacture of fertilizers and insecticides, rubber and plastic products, radio and motor-car assembly. Only one-tenth of the investment of this Plan was allocated to agriculture: a proportion far too small in a country where great opportunities both for the expansion of agriculture and, locally, its intensification are present and where food imports increase. Professor W. A. Lewis in his report on the prospects for industrial development in the Gold Coast (1953) has stated categorically:

The most certain way to promote industrialization in the Gold Coast is to lay the foundation it requires by taking vigorous measures to raise food production per person engaged in agriculture. This is the surest way of producing that large and ever-increasing demand for manufacture without which there can be little industrialization.[1]

Cocoa revenues are no longer commensurate with the widening scope and rising costs of development and the difficulty of raising the necessary capital (internally and externally) caused the second Plan to be described as an act of hope. Saving and investing are still foreign to the African's nature. Small personal incomes are not conducive to capital accumulation and if money is available better returns are obtained from trading and money-lending. Ghana would have been able to supply less than half the planned development expenditure of her moribund second Plan and the heavy loans and grants she solicited from international sources, for the separate great venture – the Volta River aluminium and hydro-electric power schemes – made it more difficult to obtain further international funds (from virtually the same bodies) for the Plan. Attempts at self-help through community development projects for secondary roads, wells, irrigation channels, etc., made some easement of demand on capital but the main problem remained.

Indeed the difficulty of raising sufficient capital and the temptation besetting the young newly independent state have been well exemplified in Ghana. The desire to maintain prestige as the first ex-colony in Africa to gain independence and to assure pan-African leadership led to the dissipation of money needed for development. Loans were made to Guinea and Mali and financial support given to various African nationalist movements. Ostentatious displays, prestige building projects, the inevitable quota of mismanagement that every young nation must expect, underlined the wasteful unreality of many projects begun under President Nkrumah. The over-ambitious Seven Year Plan, scrapped by the new government after the ousting of Nkrumah, had scarcely begun to be implemented. This plan aimed at an annual rate of economic growth of 5·5 per cent: the rate attained in 1964 was 4·5 per cent, and in 1965 fell to 3·3 per cent. The balance of payments deficit reached a record of £79 million in 1965 and loan and interest repayments on £205 million advanced in the late 1950s, mainly from overseas, were falling due 1965–6. The new government inherited a state on the verge of bankruptcy and, owing to a growing dependence on imported foodstuffs, short of many essential foods.

There is no doubt that the economic chaos into which the country had drifted by 1966 resulted from the autocratic and often high-handed methods of the former president. The disdaining of economic advice, grandiose planning with inadequate means of implementation, a proliferation of inefficient state-owned corporations ('of 37, representing an investment of £82 million, hardly one was making a profit in 1965 and few showed any promise of ever making any', *The Economist*, 5 March 1966), pre-occupation with pan-African power politics, all reduced the country's credit worthiness in international eyes. After a promising start, economic advance in Ghana had faltered.

Ghanaian governments since 1966 have adopted stringent non-inflationary policies which involved severe cut-backs on development projects and a low rate of growth. They inherited international debts of well over £200 million and the economy remained in a precarious position in the early 1970s. Since 1966 the many state-owned industries have been reorganized in the Ghana Industrial Holdings Corporation and in some cases private investment capital has been invited to assist ailing enterprises. A general problem has been the operation of many of the industries (e.g. the meat factory, jute bag manufacture, ship repairing) at well below design capacity because of import restrictions on essential raw materials and machine parts. During this period agricultural development has been stressed, with the double objective of becoming self-sufficient in food production and of providing raw materials for many of Ghana's industries.

What must be appreciated is that in both Development Plans (as in those of Nigeria) a very high proportion of expenditure has been necessary for the development of transport, communications and harbour facilities. This is partly a reflection of the antagonistic West African environment. The variation in intensity and the seasonal character of the rainfall necessitate irrigation and water conservation projects in the north, but cause serious drainage, bridging and maintenance problems in the well-watered, forested south. The heavy rainfall here is conducive to soil erosion, to the rapid deterioration of roads and helps to create conditions sympathetic to the spread of debilitating diseases. Railway and road construction in West Africa has been accomplished in the face of almost inconceivable environmental difficulties. Often the surveying of a line was the initial survey for that part of the country, valleys subject to flooding and tsetse fly had to be avoided in the rain-forest areas where the construction of innumerable bridges over streams, rivers and swamps, all with imported equipment, has required prodigious drive and very high expenditure. Ballast materials especially needed by both roads and railways in the wet south are particularly scarce there. Road builders have mainly had to use the materials they found along the line of the road, varying from sand to lateritic gravels, with a wide range of response to weather conditions. In Ghana out of 14 000 miles of motorable roads in 1970, only some 2200 miles were bitumen-surfaced. All these difficulties become translated into monetary terms when transport, communications and harbour facilities are created, and subsequently enlarge the heavy and unavoidable repair and maintenance charges. The Nigerian government estimated that the recurrent annual expenditure consequent upon the fulfilment of the 1955–60 Development Plan cost well over £4 million.

A serious problem for Ghanaian development is that her coast provides no natural site for a deep-water port. From the Ivory Coast to east of the Niger delta most of the coastline suffered submergence during the Tertiary era and has since been smoothed by the creation of sand bars from the action of south-west winds and waves and a powerful longshore drift. Tidal range is small and this coast now exhibits the double obstacles of surf and sand several hundred miles long, through which muddy rivers struggle desperately and add their own great volume of silt. In the Ivory Coast a canal was cut through the sand bar in 1907. It was badly sited and became silted up in a few months.

In 1937 because of high water in the lagoon a metre wide ditch was cut through the old choked canal to release the flood. In three days the metre ditch had a 100 metre wide mouth which in another five days had become 300 metres wide. Yet after a week the flow of water had ceased and six months later the outlet was blocked by the action of the sea.[2]

It is natural forces such as these that delay and deter harbour development, consequently with few exceptions vessels stand offshore while surf-boats ferry cargoes to and fro, a primitive and inconvenient system occasioning losses and delays.

As far back as 1928 an artificial harbour was created at Takoradi near the former unsatisfactory railhead port of Sekondi. Long breakwaters obstruct the west-to-east drift and keep clear the narrow entrance to the rectangular deep-water basin. The growing Gold Coast economy, with its export of cocoa, timber, palm oil, manganese and bauxite, by the end of the war strained the resources of this chief port and a several million pound enlargement programme was put in hand. This, completed in 1953, doubled berth capacity, mechanized the loading equipment and necessitated the removal of an eighty-foot hill covering twenty-four acres to provide level land for the siting of new railway yards and spoil for other reclamation. Except for sand, timber and aggregate from a quarry eight miles away, practically every item from cement, steel and construction plant to all-important DDT had to be sent out from Britain.

The continuing growth of Ghana's economy has led to the construction of a second deep-water port at the former fishing village of Tema, eighteen miles east of Accra and due south of the proposed Volta hydro-electric power station at Akosombo. Road, rail and water supply connections with Accra were completed in 1952 at a cost of over £3 million. The development of the port, providing deep-water berths, a dockyard, warehouses, railway sidings and marshalling yards, has been completed at a cost of £35 million. An entirely new town (pop. 108000), including an industrial area with a oil refinery, a steel mill and a large aluminium smelter, has grown beside this new port as the Volta River hydro-electric and aluminium scheme has developed.[3] The Volta River Project, which secured approval and funds from the United States in December 1961, is a major step forward in Ghanaian planned development. It comprises a £46 million aluminium smelter presently operating on imported alumina but ultimately to utilize huge local bauxite deposits, supplied with power by a £70 million hydro-electric station. The project was completed (*c*. 1968) and aluminium production for export has risen to 145 000 tons annually and the country's dependence upon cocoa is becoming much reduced.

Nigeria, also newly independent, is about four times as large as the United Kingdom or Ghana and has a population of seventy million. With a greater area and unevenly distributed population transport problems and costs are relatively greater than those of Ghana. The main concentrations of population lie in the south and the north, separated by the thinly populated 'middle belt'. An extensive network of transport and communications is needed and their cost of provision, operation and maintenance is high, irrespective of the high costs arising from varied environmental disabilities. The Six Year Development Plan begun in 1962 differed in emphasis from those of Ghana. Much stress was laid upon education, public health, agriculture, urban and rural water supplies and road development. Industry was not ignored, but the need for a firm infrastructure was appreciated; industrial development was initially steady, but cautious.

Nigerian manufacturing industry really began during the war years. In 1953 an International Bank Mission suggested various lines of industrial development, including vegetable-oil industries, such as soap and margarine manufacture, cocoa products, food canning, sack manufacture and associated fibre products, textiles, leather, wood products, cement and glass manufacture. Since then many of these industries have been established and the country now possesses cotton ginneries, plywood factories, palm-oil processing plant, breweries and factories making cement, textiles, soap, margarine and plastic goods.

The reluctance of Nigerians to forsake trade for industry where returns are less assured underlines the lack of indigenous capital. On the other hand some advance in saving habits is to be found from Post Office Savings Bank records. In 1939 there were only 42 737 accounts, whose savings totalled £185 000; in 1966 the number of accounts was 340 000 and the amount deposited totalled £3 million.

To assist in the problems of finance the government enacted the Aid to Pioneer Industries Ordinance in 1952. Under this any undertaking satisfying the condition that it is favourable to the Nigerian economy is granted a Pioneer Industry Certificate and obtains various tax reliefs. A Federal Loans Board also exists to give moderate financial aid to industrial projects. These measures have helped to bring about a marked expansion in consumer goods industries in the last five years, especially at Lagos and Port Harcourt. There are now over forty factories on the Ikeja Industrial Estate near Lagos, manufacturing such things as tyres and inner tubes, asbestos cement products, paints, beer and soft drinks.

Until recently fuel and power for industrial development in Nigeria has been limited almost entirely to the coal from Enugu. This was one reason why a major hydro-electric project, the Niger Dam at Kainji in northern Nigeria (completed in 1969), was included in the Six Year Plan. An eighth of the installed capacity has been earmarked for a proposed iron and steel plant (annual output 125000 tons of steel) to be established at Lokoja, where good-quality iron ore awaits exploitation. The use of indigenous fuel and raw materials and an inland situation (protected from imported steel by transport costs) are deemed to offset the higher costs inevitable in operating a small plant.

The fuel and power situation, however, has been radically changed during the last few years by the successful exploitation of oil and natural gas, mainly in the Niger delta. With the building of a small oil refinery near Port Harcourt and two others proposed for Warri (delta area) and Kaduna (inland) and the beginning of an internal pipeline system there is occurring a shift from the use of Enugu coal in electricity production, transport and industry to cheaper and more efficient oil and gas. Crude oil production in 1972 was over 84 million tons, and most of this was exported. The economy will benefit for many years to come, for mineral oil and natural gas are expected to be Nigeria's principal exports, and earned as much as £1800 million in 1973 – nine times the value of all Nigeria's exports in 1964.

Among the industries especially basic to development are those concerned with the creation of constructional materials. Of these the cement industry takes a paramount place yet it is rarely one of the earliest industries in a developing country. Reasons for this may be discerned from Nigeria, which now has the largest cement industry of West Africa. The industry dates only from 1957; a prime reason for its seeming leisurely promotion is that a cement works needs to be large to be economic and must be kept in full production if disproportionate rises in costs are to be avoided. A further requirement, often difficult to meet in developing countries, is for good transport facilities to assemble raw materials not *in situ* and to distribute the bulky low-value product. The post-war rise in demand for cement has now made it feasible to establish three plants in Nigeria. Cement consumption has increased from well below 100 000 tons to over half a million tons and continues to expand.

Proximity to the low-value raw materials of limestone and clay, and to the market, are important in such an industry where the product is both bulky and heavy in relation to its value and loses little weight in manufacture. Proximity to fuel deposits is less essential although an added advantage, since a modern works requires 25 tons of coal to make 100 tons of cement. The first Nigerian cement works (and the first in West Africa) was established at Nkalagu in the Eastern Region in 1957. The plant is sited near limestone and shale deposits some thirty miles from the Enugu collieries and also obtains electricity from the Oji River power station. The site was completely undeveloped and has required an eight-mile branch line and road connection to be made. The cement finds a market in the north of the Eastern Region and part of the Northern Region.

Another cement works has been erected in the Western Region between Lagos and Abeokuta, again located in relation to raw material deposits and the adjacent substantial market. This site, however, was too far from Nigeria's Enugu coalfield and only became commercially feasible with the introduction of a special manufacturing process reducing fuel requirement and utilizing fuel oil. The establishment of a third plant at Calabar has now been completed. That three regional cement factories can compete for the home market against one another and against imports may seem questionable but hopes are placed on the growing pace of the country's development (indicated by the increasing demand for constructional materials) and the careful location of the plants enjoying the protection afforded heavy, bulky low-value goods by transport costs which increase generally in direct proportion to the distance from factory to market. This results in each factory having a substantial 'protected' market area before meeting competition from its rivals or from imports.

The care with which prospective industries need to be examined before being accepted or rejected for developing countries is shown in the proposal for the manufacture of hurricane lanterns which the United Africa Co. at first thought ideally suited to West African labour and marketing conditions. Each year over one million hurricane lanterns are imported into Nigeria, paying £200000 duty. It is likely to be many years before the spread of electricity substantially reduces the market. The opportunity arose of obtaining in the United Kingdom and transferring to Nigeria an existing plant for the manufacture of hurricane lanterns. It was found that the manufacture of a hurricane lantern may require as many as 100 separate operations and that this plant consisted of a large number of small machines requiring fairly simple individual operation. This seemed advantageous to Nigerian labour conditions and with improvisation if one failed it could be by-passed: a great advantage in West Africa where local replacement of parts is often impossible. Other advantages of the project lay in the savings in freight charges and the lower import duty resulting from importing components rather than assembled lanterns. However, detailed examination suggested that the transfer of the plant to Nigeria would only pay if the whole Nigerian market could be won from the imported lanterns and that local skills could be equal to the skills available in the United Kingdom. These conditions were not likely to be met: to oust the imported lanterns it would be necessary to cut prices so much that manufacture would be unprofitable, for the far larger scale of operations in the exporting countries allowed of cheaper production. The local engineering skills, especially tool-room skills, just were not available; a background of engineering skills and tradition takes many years to build up. The project was therefore abandoned.[4]

SOUTH AMERICA: CHILE

An examination of the Huachipato iron and steel plant introduces us to Chile as a typical representative of the developing countries of South America and to the considerations and problems brought by the introduction of heavy industry in such a country. Population 'explosions' are occurring in many of South America's republics and the continent's population of about 300 million is likely to double within the next thirty years. The feudal structure of society over most of the continent explains vast differences in income per head between the two classes of society. The low average level of income, owing to the under-utilization of resources, reflects this feudal frame enclosing primary activities in relatively stagnating economies. Serious disabilities, both institutional and environmental, circumscribe and retard the development of both agriculture and industry.

In most of the South American republics as a result of war-time shortages and periodic foreign exchange crises there is already a high degree of self-sufficiency in the manufacture of such consumer goods as textiles and clothing, shoes, cigarettes, pottery and pharmaceutical and toilet preparations. A proportion of these industries has developed largely on private investment by foreign firms establishing local plants. These industries are generally tiny and exhibit high costs; their markets are relatively minute for between a half and two-thirds of the population scarcely rank as consumers. The inelasticity of demand at near subsistence level means that products of, and growth of, manufacturing industries are of little direct interest to the mass of the population. Anachronistic and inefficient systems of land tenure hold back agricultural development, but it is easier and safer for governments to plan industrial innovations than to risk political and social upheaval by instituting agrarian reforms. Consequently it is possible to find in South America numerous examples of industrial growth, yet the relative neglect of agriculture: a growing state of imbalance that may well add to, rather than decrease, the disparity of incomes. Short of revolution, which might shake the agricultural sector out of its lethargy and distribute wealth more widely, the market for consumer goods at present has few prospects of expansion. Faced with this stagnation current thought and plans for industrial expansion in the larger republics place considerable stress upon heavy industry and power production. The great hydro-electric installations and dams, the development of oil resources and establishments of refineries and petro-chemical industries, the erecting of blast furnaces and steel mills, may be ambitious acts of faith but they depend on foreign loans and grants and subsequently will demand formidable large markets. Unless the nettle is grasped and there are agrarian and social reforms and a substantial strengthening of infra-structure, a quaking, top-heavy industrial sector may well be the outcome in many South American republics.

Chile fits into this general pattern. Between 1940 and 1957 she received for capital development no less than $280 million in loans from the Export-Import Bank (Eximbank) and International Bank of Reconstruction and Development (the 'World Bank'). This money helped to further the establishment of a range of industries and services, particularly electric power, oil, coal mining, steel, cement manufacture, food processing and transport modernization. In common with many other South American states chronic inflation since the war has led to a series of financial crises (since 1953 the cost of living index has risen ten-fold). This has distorted prices, hampered economic development, widened income gaps and encouraged investment in land. The resulting stagnation of the economy was marked by an actual decline in national income after 1954 and a steady lowering of income per head as population increased. The level of investment was well below the country's needs and did not show improvement until after 1957, when a serious anti-inflation programme was adopted. The success of these measures restored the confidence of the World Bank and Eximbank, to whom the government applied for loans to develop hydro-electric power and modernize the coal industry and the railways. The lack of interest of private capital stems from the extremely limited size of the home market, for barely two-thirds of the seven and a half million population rank as consumers. Private capital concerns itself far more with mining, especially copper – the principal product upon which the economy depends. Copper, nitrates and iron ore provide the major exports and despite profits passing mainly to (usually) foreign owners, and in taxes to the government, workers in these export industries do well: for example, the Chilean copper miner earns the equivalent of $90 a week, compared with the average industrial wages of $14 a week.

The Huachipato iron and steel plant near Concepcion, opened in 1950, represents a serious attempt at diversification of the economy. Further aims of the project were to reduce the imports of foreign steel, to eliminate steel shortage, and the stimulation of new steel-using local industries. It was felt that new industrial growth and better economic stability would help to raise the general standard of living. Iron and steel lies at the base of modern industrial structure and possession of an iron and steel plant only too often may have a status symbol element. This applies less in the case of Chile, which has indigenous raw materials than, say, the St Nicholas plant in the Argentine based upon imported raw materials.

In established consumer goods industries in South America the scale of production is small, but generally so is the capital invested. The introduction of basic heavy industry such as iron and steel manufacture has been delayed in South America because even a plant of minimum economic size requires a very large investment, more than foreign investors are prepared to risk in view of the limited market potential. Chile is one of the few South American countries possessing both coal and good-quality iron ore. These are certainly 500 miles apart but both are situated near the coast and bulk transport by water is cheap. The precise location of such an industrial plant in a developing country is of outstanding importance in view of the high capital investment, for faulty location is permanent and the establishment may well remain unique in the country. Raw materials, markets, transport facilities, access to power and water, are some of the major considerations in determining the location of an iron and steel plant. The best combination of these should give lowest cost production.

Chile's integrated iron and steel works has been located on San Vicente Bay, between the port of Talcahuano and the growing town of Concepcion (Fig. 9). Sheltered deep water is adjacent to flat land where the plant has been built and a jetty permits the unloading of ore vessels from the El Romerel mine just north of Coquimbo, of limestone from the south and of cargoes of coking coal from the United States of America. Most of the coal used (65 per cent) is from mines at Lota and Schwager, twenty-five miles to the south, and is moved by rail. This coal is of high volatility and of poor coking quality and has to be mixed with imported medium volatile coal. Local coal-mining conditions are difficult and costs are high. Dolomitic limestone suitable as a blast-furnace flux is brought by sea from Guarello Island, Madre de Dios, 950 miles to the south. Dolomite with a low silica content for open-hearth furnaces has to be imported from Uruguay. The nearby rivers, Laja and Bio-Bio, provide hydro-electric power and fresh water (thirty million gallons a day are required). Labour has been available from the nearby towns of Concepcion, Talcahuano and Lota and there are road, rail and sea communications with the capital and chief town 300 miles to the north in the fertile central valley.[5]

The 'protection' afforded by transport costs of imported steel, allied to careful location permitting cheap bulk assembly of the low-value raw materials, have been the keys to Huachipato's success. Finance for the initial project came partly from the United States, Eximbank, from private foreign investors (mainly USA) and from Chilean sources. One of the conditions imposed by Eximbank was that of a managerial contract with a reputable United States firm. This contract was made with the Koppers Company and still operates although the number of Americans at the plant has been

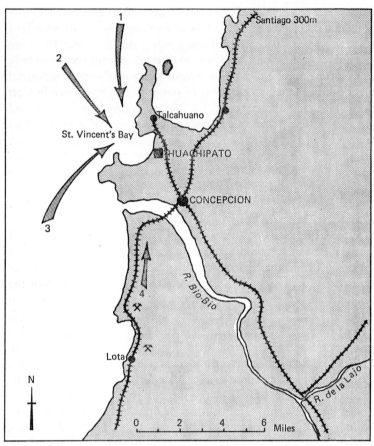

Fig. 9. The location of Huachipato: 1. Iron ore (60% Fe) and manganese (45% Mn) from Coquimbo (500 mi). 2. Coking coal (35% requirements) from USA. 3. Limestone from Madre de Dios Island (950 mi). 4. Local coking coal (65% requirements) (25 mi).

progressively reduced. The initial plant consisted of fifty-seven coke ovens, one blast furnace, one Bessemer converter, two open-hearth furnaces, a blooming mill, plate sheets and tin-plate mill. In 1954 this was expanded when thirteen more coke ovens, a second Bessemer converter and a third open-hearth furnace were added. More modern rolling plant was installed in 1956 and a fourth open-hearth furnace was added and the steel-processing plant expanded in 1959. In 1971 the plant produced 500 000 tons of pig iron and 515 000 tons of steel, as much as the domestic market could absorb. Costs of production, while higher than in the United States, still enable steel to be marketed in Chile at prices substantially below that of imports. So far the plant has benefited by being able to operate at capacity, but future expansion of the plant designed to double output by the mid-1970s is likely to show some dependence on foreign buyers. Steel-using industries in Chile have expanded notably since 1950, many plants being established around Concepcion and the steel works. New products include cars, buckets, pots and pans, pipes, wire, stoves, refrigerators, agricultural equipment.

This plant, despite its modest size the second largest in South America, is undoubtedly a successful undertaking and ranks as the most important element in Chile's industrialization in the last decade. It represents a successful utilization of indigenous resources, it has provided new industrial employment both in itself and in the new metal-using industries: it has reduced costs of steel to domestic consumers and saved foreign exchange by replacing the bulk of steel imports. It may be questioned, however, how far this enterprise has helped in the great national problem of poverty due to under-development. Was this the kind of enterprise required to revive the economy and pump fresh life into all its members?

In a sense the steel plant operates in a closed economy within the stagnating national economy. It makes profits, but most go to service the capital loaned (totalling \$153 000 000 by 1960) and to over-seas participants. The moderate lowering of steel costs has made but a very limited widening of the domestic market which remains small since the purchasing power of the mass of the population has been little affected. One is led to the conclusion that the creation of Huachipato was badly timed: its full benefits will come with an expanding purposeful economy; in itself it cannot create those conditions but the money invested in it might well have done so.

An efficient iron and steel plant attached to a small high-cost industrial sector emphasizes uneven and unbalanced development. Despite great income from mining Chile remains an agricultural country, yet her agriculture has been allowed to stagnate. For many years it has failed to keep pace with rising population so that production per head has declined, and whereas twenty years ago Chile exported more agricultural produce than she imported, now she can no longer feed herself but imports up to one-quarter of her food for her growing urban population. The system of land owner-ship inherited from the Spaniards, whereby for example 3 per cent of the landowners hold 37 per cent of the land, indicates the great gap between the rich landowner and the labourer or peasant. Many landowners prefer to live in Santiago than at their enormous haciendas and much cultivable land remains as rough grazing. Government price policies and inflation whereby land was bought as a defence against monetary devaluation rather than for cultivation have aided this situation.

Since 1940 Chile's population has grown annually by about 2·0 per cent, whereas per capita production of food has increased annually by only 0·6 per cent. The root of Chile's poverty and under-development lies in her agricultural sector. Land-reform legislation removing anachronistic tenure systems, reducing the under-productive large estates and sharing the land (and thus much of the national income) more equally, associated with investment in irrigation, communications and services, pumps and agricultural equipment would seem the logical first stages to any planned development. In the face of the all-powerful landowning aristocracy little progress on these lines was possible until a socialist government came to power in 1970 and forced land-reform measures on reluctant large landowners. This was long overdue and was strongly opposed and was a factor in the subsequent overthrow of the government. In the past a moderate industrial development has been easier to achieve, in Chile's case a plunge into basic capital-intensive industry theoretically making possible a subsequent upsurge in consumer goods production when demand becomes effective, but in fact having a limited effect upon the country's human and economic problems.

HONG KONG

The economic development of Hong Kong since the war provides a salutary example of a people lifting themselves by their own bootstraps. Their achievements deserve the widest publicity among other developing countries. The Colony consists of the island of Hong Kong (29 sq. miles), the tip of Kowloon peninsula on the mainland ($3\frac{1}{2}$ sq. miles) and the adjacent New Territories leased from China until 1998 ($365\frac{1}{2}$ sq. miles). The New Territories comprise the mainland section north of Kowloon and over 200 islands and islets. Most of the area is mountainous and barren, with only 13 per cent of the land under crops or livestock. In 1931 the population was about 850000, but by 1947 it was estimated at 1800000.

Today, after years of Chinese immigration, the total population is over 4 million, most of it being crowded into an urban area of 12 sq. miles. Not only has Hong Kong received thousands of immigrants from China, but her own crude death rate has fallen to as little as 5 per thousand of the population (one of the lowest in the world); however, former high crude birth rates have moderated to around 20 per thousand and the rate of natural increase, once one of the highest in the world, is now more manageable. The social and economic problems implicit in such a situation were made worse by the changes forced upon the island's economy by the Chinese revolution. Before the war Hong Kong existed on entrepôt trade: it served all Far Eastern countries but the greater part of its business was with China for whom it took on the attributes of a huge shop. Today the volume of trade with China is much smaller and new markets have had to be found in such countries as Malaya, Indonesia, Japan, East Africa, the USA and the United Kingdom. A further change is that the majority of the exports are of goods manufactured in Hong Kong. The Colony has been transformed from a trading into an industrial economy.

The decision to further manufacturing industry was the only one possible after the war. The rapidly growing population, considerably swollen by Chinese refugees, could not be fed from local production and there were few resources and services with which to pay for food imports amounting to seven-eighths of total consumption. The Colony was in the unenviable position of having virtually no raw materials, fuel or power with which to develop industry and could only capitalize her two major resources of position in relation to world seaways and trade and an abundant supply of cheap labour. No other country in the world has fought and overcome such handicaps, for even Japan was not utterly destitute of raw materials and fuel. Hong Kong's success, whereas many other Asian countries facing similar problems have made little progress, in no small measure is due to the character and quality of the people.

Nearly all the workers and most of the entrepreneurs are Chinese who have a world-wide reputation for diligence, perseverance and thrift. They are dexterous and skilful and quick to learn, and shrewd in perceiving opportunities. Some private saving goes abroad, often to families left in China. The rest becomes invested in the Colony, in tools and machinery or as public saving of which the government has made wise use in building up utilities. Inevitably there has been a certain amount of unemployment and this has tempered wage demands to reasonable limits.

In the immediate post-war years, when a mass of refugees swarmed into the Colony, cheap and plentiful labour was a mainstay of Hong Kong's economic growth. Wages are still low by European standards, but not by general Asian standards. Wages paid in the textile industry are nearly double those paid in India, Pakistan and Taiwan. Hong Kong rates also represent low labour costs, because the productivity of the labour is high. Daily working hours are limited to a maximum of ten for women and young persons (14–18), but there are no restrictions on working hours for men. In fact, three-quarters of the men employed in industry work ten hours a day or less.

Szczepanik, in his study of Hong Kong's development, demolishes the notion that the Colony thrives on sweated and half-starved labour. He adds:

> If it is considered that the cost of simple food in Hong Kong is much cheaper, and that the warm climate does not require such a large calorie intake as in Britain, it could be concluded that the industrial revolution in Hong Kong was not taking place at the expense of the standards of nutrition. The Hong Kong worker, moreover, was spending much less on smoking than the British worker, and the geographical limitation of the Colony's area did not require so much to be spent on transport as in Britain. The main hardships of Hong Kong workers are to be found in the very low housing standards.

He goes on to show that the standard of living of the Hong Kong industrial worker is much higher than that of his counterpart in China and points to the inflow of economic immigrants (apart from political refugees) attracted by better conditions and the more humanitarian character of Hong Kong's industrial revolution.

> The economic system of Hong Kong, with its powerful mechanism of competition which keeps all prices low, not only enables the workers to maintain a fairly decent standard of living, but also permits an average family to save some 2·35 per cent of its monthly earnings and, to send another part of these earnings to relatives in China.[6]

Foremost among the circumstances helpful to the Colony's development is its geographical position, which led to the growth of a great port with associated repair and servicing facilities, able to offer certain external economies to new industry. Such a port has banking, finance and insurance facilities and commercial connections with suppliers and potential customers all over the world. The very concentration of industry into so limited an area adds to the scale of external economies that accrued and to the scope and efficiency of the public utilities. The stable government, law and order, and absence of corruption attracted both the entrepreneur and the investor, many being Chinese refugees who did not come into the Colony destitute and who were prepared to risk their capital in new manufactures and new methods, ever seeking new markets. They were favoured by low rates of taxation, a measure of Commonwealth Preference, but no tariff protection, special concessions or subsidies from the government.

In twenty-five years Hong Kong's 800 factories have multiplied to over 5000 and more than 800000 are employed in industry. The range of manufactures has expanded markedly and they now account for 80 per cent of the Colony's exports. Heavy industry is restricted to shipbuilding, repairing and ship-breaking (Hong Kong is the world's largest ship-breaking centre). Over half the scrap from broken-up ships is exported to Japan, but also the Colony's growing steel-rolling mills are supplied; they produce reinforcing rods and bars, some for export. Textiles form the largest manufacturing industry (over 750000 spindles, employing more than 55000 workers). Cotton, rayon, silk and woollen yarns are spun, woven, knitted, dyed and printed and all types of garment and textile goods produced. The spinning mills are among the most up-to-date in the world; much of the plant had been ordered, after the war, for Shanghai, but deteriorating conditions there allowed Hong Kong to take delivery. Textiles accounted for 50 per cent of exports by value in 1972. Other manufactures include enamelware (mainly for African and Southeast Asian markets), vacuum flasks, electric torches, batteries, transistor products, metal goods such as hurricane lanterns, stoves, lamps, nails, metal windows, zip fasteners; footwear, rubber and leather goods, plastic ware, especially toys and artificial flowers; wig-making, printing and publishing and cement manufacture (only the clay being a local raw material).

The Colony is now moving from the stage where it relies upon low-wage industries to give it competitiveness; it has broadened its range of products and introduced new and advanced technologies. Units of production have become larger, more research and innovation is now taking place. Newer industries include the manufacture of machine tools and steel tableware, while the electronics industry has expanded to include the manufacture of memory cores for computers and complete television sets. During the last decade the tourist industry has expanded markedly and more than a million tourists (one-third from Japan) visit the Colony annually.

The far-flung trade connections of the Colony have been of benefit but she has been assiduous in seeking out and fostering overseas markets, attending Trade Fairs all over the world, sending out trade missions, pushing her wares persistently and so successfully that old-established industrial centres such as Lancashire have recently cried out for discrimination against her imports. In the case of Lancashire this has resulted in an agreed voluntary reduction of exports of grey cloth from Hong Kong to Britain. The United States has also sought a voluntary reduction of exports of grey cloth, while Australia has limited imports of rubber footwear, Benelux of gloves, while Kenya and Uganda have imposed steep import duties on enamelware in order to protect local industry, a form of discrimination that must be expected throughout Africa and South-east Asia as young manufacturing industries develop. France as a member of the European Common Market has also abrogated her liberal trade policies regarding Hong Kong textiles. In short, a new phase is occurring: as one critic has put it 'because her competition was too effective'. One secret of Hong Kong's success is that neither capital nor labour is allowed to be left idle. According to a survey in 1957 Hong Kong spindles operated for 8522 hours out of a year's total of 8784 hours. In contrast Indian spindles worked only 5602 hours, German 3729 hours and Lancashire only 1526 hours.

These developments, the negation of the 'trade, not aid' theme which Hong Kong has vigorously espoused, must not blind us to the Colony's astounding industrial progress. Such a virile community does not let the pace of development flag. The scarcity of water and suitable land for industrial purposes are current difficulties being surmounted by water conservation schemes and the levelling of hills and use of the spoil to reclaim land from the sea. One scheme at Kwun Tong in Kowloon Bay has already reclaimed 58 acres (for twenty-two new factories) and a further 177 acres is being provided. An industrial town of a quarter of a million people has been created there. Another scheme in the New Territories, now well under way, envisages comprehensive development over fifteen years on an area to include much offshore and bay reclamation. The programme covers some 6000 acres in the Tsuen Wan area, and of this 711 acres are destined for industry[7]. Land, however, becomes more expensive, a serious matter since cost of land has always been a greater proportion of final cost of an industrial unit than is normal elsewhere.

Labour, too, is likely to become more expensive and Hong Kong's competitive advantage may become less pronounced during the present decade.

In many respects the unique character of Hong Kong's material and human situation has forced development along limited channels. She has succeeded in avoiding starvation for her growing millions by successful industrialization, whereby she realized her two great advantages of low wage rates and high productivity of labour. The limitations of her situation and resources has brought the classic response of fabricating raw materials that are light relative to their value and that require little fuel in the manufacture. We now have the abnormal situation of a developing country living by the export of manufactures. The lesson to be appreciated by other developing countries, especially of Asia, is that the activities creating the links in this chain of development were not automatic and of mystical origin but have become reality thanks to the efforts, exertion and driving force of a dedicated, disciplined and perceptive people.

BIBLIOGRAPHICAL REFERENCES

1. W. A. Lewis, *Report on Industrialization and the Gold Coast* (Accra, 1953), p. 2.

2. R. J. Harrison Church, 'The Sea in West African Development', *West Africa* (1951), p. 74.

3. D. Hilling, 'Tema – the geography of a new port', *Geography* (1966), pp. 111–25.

4. United Africa Co., *Statistical and Economic Review,* No. 23 (1959), p. 20.

5. C. L. White and R. H. Chilcote, 'Chile's New Iron and Steel Industry', *Economic Geography* (1961), pp. 258–66.

6. E. Szczepanik, *The Economic Growth of Hong Kong* (London, 1958), pp. 71–2.

7. D. C. Y. Lai and D. J. Dwyer, 'Tsuen Wan: A new industrial town in Hong Kong', *Geog. Rev.* (1964), pp. 151–69.

M. Darkoh, 'The distribution of manufacturing in Ghana', *Scottish Geog. Mag.* (1971), pp. 38–57.

A. Hay, 'Imports versus local production: A case study from the Nigerian cement industry', *Econ. Geog.* (1971), pp. 384–8.

F. J. Pedler, *Economic Geography of West Africa* (London, 1955).

F. Benham and H. Holley, *The Economy of Latin America* (New York, 1946).

F. Benham, 'The Growth of Manufacturing in Hong Kong', *International Affairs* (1956), pp. 456–63.

B. H. Farmer, 'The Ceylon Ten-Year Plan, 1959–68', *Pacific Viewpoint* (1961), pp. 123–36.

W. Baer, 'Regional inequality and economic growth in Brazil', *Economic Development and Cultural Change* (1964), pp. 268–85.

R. Clark, *Aid in Uganda – Programmes and Policies*, ODI (London, 1966).

G. Benveniste and W. E. Moran, *Handbook of African Development* (New York, 1962).

9 The progress of industrialization
II. India; Egypt

No other under-developed, vast and populous country, with the exception of Communist China, is struggling for development in so determined a fashion as India. The problems being overcome are multitudinous and massive. Both India and China are launched on a series of Five Year Plans, but of very different character. India's aim is to raise standards generally and increase consumption by an all-round economic development and not to create a monolithic industrial state. Whereas in India's first Plan agriculture and irrigation were earmarked 31 per cent of funds and industry and power 19 per cent, in China no less than 58 per cent was allotted to heavy industry, only 7·6 per cent to irrigation and nothing at all to agriculture. India plans a welfare state by humane methods, based upon the co-operation of a free people, but China aims at rapidly becoming a world power by regimented labour and compulsory savings. India's efforts and progress are watched sympathetically by the Western world: in some senses ideologies are on trial. Economists are particularly eager to watch the first application on a massive scale in a non-Communist country of the relatively new theory of economic growth.

India's economy appears to have stagnated over a considerable period. The occupational structure of the population scarcely altered during the first half of the century, for in 1911 it was estimated that 71 per cent of the working population was engaged in agriculture while in 1948 the proportion was 68 per cent. The population grew by 52 per cent in the half-century (1901 census 235·5 million, 1951 census 365·9 million), but the expansion of the economy lagged; the sown area per person declined and yields did not increase. Sir John Russell suggests that the deterioration of the dietary had begun before the 1930s, although strictly comparable data are lacking to confirm this.[1] Under-employment in rural areas has reached chronic proportions: poverty, disease and famine have come to be regarded as the traditional lot of the Indian peasantry.

F

A policy of protection commencing in 1922 favoured the growth of a small industrial sector and the shortages during the Second World War gave India's young industries a further fillip. Textiles, iron and steel, cement and sugar manufacture were among the major industries at the time of independence and partition (1947) and a large amount of workshop or cottage industry existed. Modern type industry, however, only gave employment to 2·4 million workers. Precise data regarding per capita income are lacking, but estimates for 1948–9 put it at about £20 per head.

India's utter poverty is best demonstrated briefly by certain statistics. The degree of literacy despite determined remedial efforts is barely 28 per cent; there are only 96000 doctors and 25000 hospital beds among a population of 570 million. Some 82 per cent of the population is rural and most of India's 500000 villages are still primitive in that pure-water supply, sewerage, drainage and electricity are hardly known there. The grinding poverty of the masses, with their lives of leisurely toil, their unvarying and insufficient diet, often still at the mercy of the landlord or village usurer, all enveloped in a decaying caste system, served to multiply the difficulties for the government to whom the Indian people traditionally look for succour and guidance. An Indian Finance Minister said recently, regarding the third Five Year Plan: 'We cannot afford to make a slip for our capacity to pay for our follies is very limited.' This may well apply also to the Indian peasant who lives at near-starvation level; with so little margin he dare not run risks by varying his traditional husbandry. To sap this solid wall of rural conservatism is a task demanding time, and that the planners are being denied.

A particular feature about the first fifteen years of India's planned development, taken as axiomatic by the planning commission, was a pronounced emphasis within the industrial sector on heavy, basic capital-intensive industries such as steel, coal, oil, power and chemicals. The rigorous implementation of these views has divided Western economists. Many believe, and events seem to support them, that much more investment should be made in agriculture, transport and education before heavy expenditure on steel mills, but others support the views of the Indian planners, pointing out that in many respects India stands apart from the majority of developing countries.[2] India has large reserves of some of the richest iron ores in the world (over 60 per cent Fe), manganese, coal, bauxite and mica. There is a large potential of hydro-electric power and oil prospecting is now meeting with some success. India's plans, influenced by these endowments and the knowledge that industrialization has the major role in securing rapid economic advance, have favoured capital-intensive projects because of the narrow base of the existing industrial sector, with little development of basic and heavy industry that provide the foundations on which manufacturing industries depend. It is felt that India's potential to produce steel, aluminium, chemicals and other basic materials relatively cheaply must be realized as rapidly as possible although the amount of investment required in such plants is tremendous and the initial return and numbers employed are relatively small. As has been pointed out earlier, the application of such policies requires a degree of discipline and fortitude in the population: a belief that by having no jam today at least some will become available tomorrow.

Despite India's emphasis upon basic heavy industries she nevertheless makes provision for fostering cottage and small-scale industry. Their claimed advantages to her economy at its present stage are that they use more labour and less capital per unit of output than large industry and that small industries are a useful means of dispersal of industry. Further, they decentralize economic power and distribute income more evenly. Cottage establishments are largely centred on the village and use labour-intensive techniques to make traditional goods. These are now joined by small factory enterprises using power and modern production techniques and making products new to India such as umbrellas, torches, aluminium utensils and sewing machines. Aided by import restrictions and government help by means of loans and hire-purchase finance for the buying of machinery, these are growing in numbers and have become a major supplier of consumption goods. As the programme advances some of the earlier premises seem less valid. Recent studies have shown that the smaller enterprise does not always save capital; quite often small factories use not merely more labour but also more capital per unit of output. They usually have relatively more unused capacity than larger plants and seldom work more than one shift. Also the need for external economies prevents their widespread dispersal among villages.[3] Nevertheless sentiment is strong for sustaining such industries and the growth of these new small enterprises is bringing into being the all-important class of go-ahead industrialists and entrepreneurs, emerging from diverse social and economic backgrounds.

India's charted course to development began with her first Five Year Plan in 1951, was continued in her second Plan in 1956 and then by the third Plan, 1961–6. The fourth Plan, nominally 1966–70, had its commencement delayed three years owing to the economic crisis related to the brief war with Pakistan and the failure of the monsoons 1965–7. The broad allocation of both public and private development investment is given in Tables 9 and 10, and the magnitude of India's task is mirrored in their totals: £2500 million, £5060 million, £7800 million and £14250 million. Each plan becomes more gigantic to sustain the momentum of its predecessor, and the returns expected at first sight might appear very modest. This is a reflection of the enormous investment in services necessary to establish an infra-structure of the size and scale deemed necessary to support and sustain the industrial growth of a sub-continent.

The first Five Year Plan was designed to increase the national income by 13 per cent and to raise the proportion of investment to national income from a traditional 5 per cent to 7 per cent. Much emphasis was laid on public utilities, services, and on agricultural development. Power, transport, communications, education and health absorbed 55 per cent of the £1500 million of the public sector's outlay, while irrigation and agriculture took 31 per cent. Industry and mining rightly received a low priority. The plan was based upon an expected capital : output ratio of 3 : 1, a proportion deemed reasonable for developing countries by most economists. The Plan proved far more successful than had been anticipated; the modest targets were more than achieved, good monsoons contributed bumper crops and national income rose by 18·4 per cent and the capital : output ratio proved to be a remarkably good 1·8 : 1. The second Plan, 1956–61, was less successful; the planners had become over-optimistic. It was intended that the national income should rise by 25 per cent at the end of the Plan period and the rate of investment to national income to go up from 7 per cent to 11 per cent. The capital : output ratio estimate was increased to 2·3 : 1, a rate that proved to be too optimistic. This plan reduced the public investment proportion in agriculture and irrigation and allocated a total of nearly £1800 million as public investment in industrial development, transport and communications.

The emphasis upon heavy industrial investment saw substantial developments in the Damodar Valley, Calcutta's hinterland in West Bengal and Bihar (Fig. 10). Here in 1948 had been established the Damodar Valley Corporation, based upon the pattern of the

Table 9: *Outlay and investment in India's Five Year Plans, 1951–74*

	(£ Million)				
Sector	*First plan 1951–6*	*Second plan 1956–61*	*Total 1956–61*	*Third plan 1961–6*	*Fourth plan 1969–74*
Public sector outlay	1470	3450	4920	5625	10875
Public sector investment	1170	2737	3907	4725	9000
Private sector investment	1350	2325	3675	3075	5250
Total investment	2520	5062	7582	7800	14250

SOURCE: Govt. of India, Planning Commission, *Third Five Year Plan*, New Delhi, 1961, p. 32; *Fourth Five Year Plan – Resources, Outlays and Programmes*, New Delhi, 1965, p. 4.

Table 10: *India's Five Year Plans 1951-74*

Distribution of plan outlay by major heads of development (Public Sector)

	(£ Million)							
Head	*First plan expenditure %*		*Second plan expenditure %*		*Third plan expenditure %*		*Fourth plan expenditure %*	
Agriculture and community dev.	218	15	398	11	801	14	1900	18
Irrigation	233	16	315	9	488	9	695	6
Power	195	13	334	10	759	13	1375	13
Industry and mining	88	6	806	24	1338	24	2450	22
Transport and communications	392	27	975	28	1114	20	2075	19
Social services and miscellaneous	344	23	622	18	1125	20	2380	22
Total	1470	100	3450	100	5625	100	10875	100
	(actual)		(actual)		(actual)		(anticipated)	

SOURCE: Govt. of India, Planning Commission, *Third Five Year Plan*, New Delhi, 1961, p. 58; *Fourth Five Year Plan – Resources, Outlays and Programmes*, New Delhi, 1965, pp. 4–5.

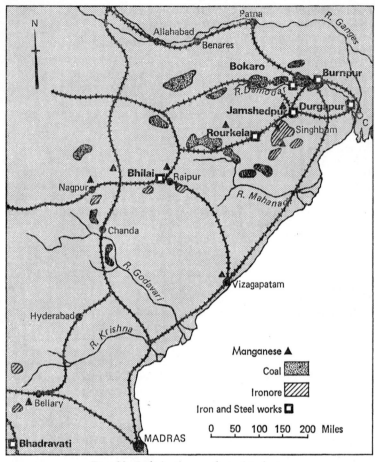

Fig. 10. India's iron and steel industry.

TVA, with a programme of electric-power production, flood control and soil conservation.[4] New coal mines now supplement pre-war workings and the great Jamshedpur iron and steel plant of the private Tata group was enlarged and new plants established by the government, such as those at Durgapur, Bhilai and Rourkela built by British, Russian and German groups. Fertilizer and chemical works and commercial vehicle manufacturing plant, locomotive and cable works also became established in this favourable setting. The electric power supplied by the Damodar authority to industry and to Calcutta Corporation quadrupled between 1956 and 1961.

Immense strides were made in laying industrial foundations and creating great capital-intensive basic plants.

The plan, however, ran into great difficulties and was only saved after the almost complete exhaustion of foreign reserves by substantial foreign aid. The planners had made insufficient allowance for monsoonal variability which reduced harvests, and for the rate of increase of population which contributed to the necessity to import food. The plan was based upon an estimated rate of population growth of 1·25 per cent per annum; in fact the rate of population increase grew during the decade and by the end of the plan was as high as 2 per cent per annum. A limited scaling-down of estimates became necessary and at the end of the five years food production totalled 75 million tons against a target of 80 million tons; only 2·6 million tons of finished steel was produced although installed capacity had risen to 4 500 000 tons. Coal production was 53 million tons against a target of 60 million tons. National income rose by 20 per cent instead of 25 per cent. Eight million new jobs had been created but ten million new workers had queued for them and a backlog of several million unemployed remained.

Nevertheless, at the end of the first decade (the 1950s) of planned development some notable advances had been made. Some £7500 million had been invested in the national economy. The national income, at constant prices, rose by 42 per cent; allowing for population growth of 82 million and fresh investment this meant a per capita increase of 20 per cent in income and 16 per cent in consumption. The agricultural sector productivity increased by 40 per cent, and 20 million more acres came under irrigation. Basic and capital goods industry expanded eight-fold. Nitrogenous fertilizer production (in terms of nitrogen) increased from 9000 to 150 000 tons per annum and bicycle production from 100 000 to 1 050 000 per year. Power-generating capacity increased from 2300 MW to 5800 MW. A definite momentum had been attained and in the private sector the beginning of an entrepreneurial class could be recognized.

The third Plan (1961–6) aimed at sustaining and accelerating this momentum, at the same time profiting by the mistakes of the second Plan. Agriculture was upgraded to receive almost as much investment as industry. The emphasis on basic industries producing investment goods continued and considerable restraint on consumer goods industries remained. It was hoped to raise the rate of investment to national income to 14 per cent (and 16 per cent by 1970). An increase of at least 5 per cent in the national income was aimed at by 1966, the rate of population increase had been estimated at 2 per cent per annum and the planned capital : output ratio was 2·62 : 1. Unfortunately, from many points of view India's third Plan was a failure. Its beginning was marred and impeded by the Chinese aggression and the necessity to increase expenditure on defence, and also by poor monsoons. At mid-Plan Mr Nehru's illness and death removed a firm influence and a leader of international stature. Towards the close, war with Pakistan and another poor monsoon upset the economy and brought near-famine conditions in several provinces. Above all this, the rate of population increase grew steadily and by 1964 was 2·5 per cent per annum: once again a much higher rate than had been planned for. Of particular disappointment was the tardy return from the great basic industrial complexes: iron and steel plants, great hydro-electric plants, petro-chemical works, shipyards, etc., great projects that had over fifteen years absorbed immense capital sums but still contributed little to the balance of payments or to the standard of living of the mass of the people. It had been hoped that by the end of the third Plan the new heavy engineering and machine building capacity would enable much capital equipment previously imported to be made in India, and that new basic raw materials for the maintenance of many industries would be made in India and replace imports, e.g. of rayon, synthetic rubber, organic chemicals, intermediates for dyestuffs and the drug industries. Some progress was made, but the high hopes were not borne out.

In terms of achievement, agriculture reached barely 85 per cent of the target of self-sufficiency in food grains, and only 80 per cent of the planned expansion of irrigation was achieved. Installed electricity capacity reached 10 300 M W whereas the target was 12 700 M W. Iron and steel production reached 13·6 million tons against a target of 16·7 million tons. Artificial fertilizer production barely reached 500 000 tons instead of a planned 856 000 tons. Mining and mineral production did better. A Bureau of Mines was established in 1948 and the Geological Survey of India was expanded in 1951 to allow a systematic investigation into India's mineral potentialities. These investigations began to bear fruit in the second Plan, with increasing outputs of coal, bauxite and iron ore. The establishment of new coal mines or expansion of existing collieries is now occurring, particularly in Bengal-Bihar, Andhra Pradesh, Madhya Pradesh and Orissa. New copper mines with concentrating and smelting plant are planned for the Khetri area of Rajasthan and other deposits are now worked at Rangpo in Sikkim. Iron ore production (10 million tons in 1960) increased two-and-a-half times when new mines, mainly in Orissa, were completed during the third Plan and allow 10 million tons of iron ore to be exported annually. Much of it goes to Japan which is providing technical assistance in establishing the new mines.

In all, during the Plan period new employment was created for thirteen millions. However, seventeen new millions were seeking jobs. With all these efforts, however, average income per head did not rise above about £26 per annum, that is a rise of £2. In India a sense of stagnation and frustration accompanied by much heart-searching attended the last months of the third Plan. A number of the self-criticisms rendered Indian economists and planners more receptive of the views increasingly voiced by outside observers and creditor nations: that agriculture must receive marked priority; that the type of industrial development must ease away from the capital-intensive pattern; that all-out efforts must be made to reduce the fertility of the population, that the planning is too rigid and bureau-cratic, and that the private sector must be given a greater part to play, especially if foreign capital is to be attracted. These views influenced the pattern of the fourth Plan which, by investments of over £14000 million, aimed at an annual growth of national income of 6·5 per cent. The proportions of investment are shown in Table 10. A much greater sum was allotted to the improvement and expansion of agriculture, with the intention of raising the annual output by 5 per cent. Emphasis on heavy industry was reduced, although one new steel plant (built at Bokara with Russian aid) was included. Infra-structure investment on power and transport was not cut, but was aimed to support agriculture, with new rural roads, rather than industry. A large part (£3000 million) of the enormous cost of the fourth Plan depended on foreign help; the tremendous investment needed being quite beyond India's own resources.

The inception of this plan was delayed by the war with Pakistan and severe droughts in 1966 and 1967. Three annual Plans filled the gap. The fourth Plan also suffered from the further war with Pakistan over the secession of Bangladesh and, like all the Plans except the first, it has failed to reach its targets. The outline of the fifth Plan (1974–9), with a total investment of nearly £30000 million and a growth target of 5·5 per cent a year has been approved by the Indian government. This plan envisages an increase of steel production from 5·8 million tons (1973–4) to 9·4 million tons (1978–9), and of artificial fertilizer from 2 million tonnes to 5·1 million tons. A

G

significant growth of agricultural production is aimed at in which it is hoped that new strains of high-yielding rice will give impetus to the Green Revolution that already has doubled India's wheat yield within a decade.

A number of features discussed in earlier chapters have become apparent in Indian development; the foremost among them is the need for, and the massive problem of, land reform. It was recognized that the inherited agrarian structure was an impediment to progress and the system of landownership and tenancies a source of exploitation of the peasantry. Measures have been included in development plans to abolish intermediary or 'rent-receiving' tenures; to regulate and reduce rents and offer security of tenure leading to the conferment of the right of ownership on tenants. A ceiling was placed on future acquisition of land by individuals and some attempts were made to consolidate fragmented holdings. The long-term aim of these measures is to convert the majority of India's cultivators into peasant-proprietors. The drawback of small-scale production and marketing will be met by the encouragement of voluntary co-operatives for credit, marketing, processing and distributing. Unfortunately the various agrarian reform laws have been honoured more in the breach than in the observance, and the current Green Revolution is making the issue of growing importance. The Green Revolution is an outcome of modernization and acceptance of new techniques (as well as high-yielding seeds) by a part of India's farmers. These are both receptive and well-to-do, and now include men of commerce and industry who have money to invest in farming. Private irrigation schemes, tractors and other mechanical appliances, the use of fertilizers and pesticides, the acceptance of the advice of agricultural officers, are the hallmarks of these new-style farmers. The benefits of the Green Revolution have been unevenly distributed and it is the well-to-do and richer peasants who have gained most. A split is occurring in India's agricultural society.

In the industrial sector a feature some observers have commented on is the tendency for production costs to be high by world standards. To some degree one may expect young industries to have higher than average costs during the teething period, but there are a number of features suggesting that a dangerously high cost structure is being created. The early pace of development exceeded India's limited supply of technical, administrative and managerial talent. Building and bringing into operation three large steel plants simultaneously proved an enormous task, a major problem being lack of experienced staff, for each plant needed about two thousand trained men. The government hurriedly recruited 1436 engineers, to be trained for the steel industry in India and abroad. But it was soon realized that the only solution to the problem of manning the three steel plants lay in recruitment of technicians from abroad. Large-scale industry in the private sector is still aided by European management, but much public sector industry relies for management upon experienced senior civil servants and railway officials who become remarkably ineffective when translated to manage steel or fertilizer plants or mines. One result is ministerial interference, even with industrial management, while industrial costs and prices increasingly become the concern of the Comptroller and Auditor General.[5] Management is thus hampered and the effects penetrate adversely throughout the system.

In a country the size of India with its limited transport net, faulty industrial location can have crucial bearing upon industrial costs, and the temptation to ignore purely economic considerations in deciding locations is very high, for every part of the federal union clamours for the attention of the Central Government in demanding the seeds of development. Some preference has been given to the location of public sector projects in relatively backward areas 'whenever this could be done without significant prejudice to technical and economic considerations'.[6] Political insistence in some cases may well have overridden efficiency and certainly causes delays in implementing plans. Other dangers appeared in the third Plan, which included a nuclear power station near Bombay and the development of a state oil industry. It is questionable whether either is necessary at this stage. Bombay power shortage might be met by modern efficient thermal electric stations supplying a super-grid more economically than by a relatively high-cost nuclear reactor. Also the increasing need for oil products can be met more speedily and cheaply by the established international companies.

A number of features may be stressed in considering India's planned development. The first we have already met and continues to be fundamental; it is the vital necessity to develop agriculture both to complement and sustain an industrial sector. Indian agriculture is particularly susceptible to weather (i.e. the monsoons) influences and this the planners miscalculated. They also seem to have moved industrial investment to first priority too soon, only to be caught out by bad harvests and an unexpectedly large population increment to feed and 'service'. The government's predilection for massive investment in capital goods industries is open to criticism. The need for increased food production is paramount and exports earning foreign exchange desirable. There is a case for investment in heavy industry to be scaled down to allow more investment in agriculture, light industry (some of its products being exportable) and education. This, however, is tantamount to saying that in its details no such great social and economic experiment can expect to obtain unanimous and unqualified support.

Secondly, the success of this notable exercise in planned development has been jeopardized by a rate of population increase far higher than had been expected. While more accurate counting is one contributive cause, others undoubtedly have been due to small dietary improvements and to the effects of infra-structure expenditure on medicine and hygiene whereby the crude death rate (especially the infant mortality rate) has fallen. From 1947 to 1957 the infant mortality rate fell from 146 to 100 per thousand live births, while by 1970 the crude death rate had fallen from 27·4 to 16·7 per thousand of the population. At the present rate of population increase almost fifteen million new mouths must be fed each year. Despite the vast scale of plans not enough work has yet been provided for the annual new entrants to the labour market, a situation that will become critical when the 'bulge' of recent births reach the labour market during the 1970s; a factor that may well delay the 'take-off'.

With the unexpected rise in the rate of population increase a special urgency attaches to the consideration of the provision of employment. During the second Plan opportunities were provided in new employment for around eight million, of which some 6·5 million were outside agriculture. At the end of the Plan period the backlog of unemployment was estimated at eight million. In addition estimates put under-employed at up to eighteen million. The third Plan may have created up to fourteen or fifteen million new jobs (10·5 million non-agricultural) but the labour force increased by seventeen million; so far in each plan the provision of new jobs has fallen short of the labour-force increment. Thus the fourth Plan started with a backlog of unemployed nearing twelve million and had to cater for a twenty-five million addition to the labour force during 1969–74. Calculations show that increase in the labour force during the next decade from 1960 may be around sixty million, comprising twenty-five millon in the fourth and thirty-five million in the fifth Plan. These figures show the immensity of India's problems and a measure of her achievement. Faith needs to be put in the cumulative character of development, especially bearing in mind the current emphasis on capital-intensive basic industries offering great promise of expansion of manufacturing industries in years to come. Nevertheless, it seems questionable whether a self-sustaining growth economy will be achieved during this decade. Population is the very crux of India's problems and unless the birth rate soon shows an appreciable fall long-term prospects are rather dispiriting. That population growth can vitiate the most strenuous efforts at development was recognized in the third Plan, where no less than £18·75 million was allocated to family planning and birth control, but with the high level of illiteracy and little public interest behind the family-planning programme results will be slow. No less than £71 million was allocated for this purpose in the fourth Plan. Population projections made in connection with the fourth Plan were 1971, 560 million; 1976, 630 million.

The third noteworthy feature is the enormous scale of investment necessary when dealing with a country of subcontinental size and population. This suggests that the huge foreign aid should be by means of grants or loans at a low rate of interest, otherwise payment of debt liabilities will create an intolerable strain upon the emergent economy. It is noteworthy that the foreign aid required for the fourth Plan was estimated at £3000 million, but no less than £1015 million of this was earmarked for the repayment or servicing of earlier loans. The mass of India's population is still little aware of the enormous efforts being made on its behalf. Often it resists the innovations demanded by the planners: general support and understanding are not great. Even the measures of land reform have had less impact than had been expected: collusion and evasion at lower levels have been widespread and a proper understanding of the integral part of land reform in development plans is rarely realized. To some degree this may be that the fruits of twenty-five years of planning have scarcely reached the peasant, for whereas national income has increased by two-thirds the population has grown by 200 million and income per head has risen by only about £5 from £21 to £26, a small return for such large efforts due to rigorous control of consumption and the sheer weight of numbers sharing the increase.

Despite two decades of tremendous effort and unprecedented investment the Indian economy is only just on the move. To prise it from rest, to overcome massive inertia, has required a heavy mobilization and application of human and material resources, for development on such a scale requires a whole range of problems and difficulties to be overcome. In the industrial field definite gains have been made, although there has as yet been no radical change in the structure of the economy nor in the condition of the mass of the population. An inadequate use of capacity raises costs in much of India's public sector industries. These are mainly sophisticated plants demanding more skilled labour and needing a higher degree of managerial strength and expertise than is available at present. Because of the low use of capacity the capital : output ratio in the heavy industries of the public sector is as high as six to one. Valuable experience has been won; particularly it has been found that the gestation period of an industrial project, especially in heavy engineering, is longer than generally expected. Many plants (iron and steel, fertilizers and chemicals) are being completed a year to two years after the target date and teething troubles reduce early output so much that many projects expected to make a valuable contribution to the third Plan only started to make a substantial contribution in the fourth. The slowly broadening base of India's industrial structure during the past twenty-five years, and a growing efficiency in production, may well lessen the balance of payments problems during the fifth Plan and facilitate the growth of exports. However, so long as population growth continues at the current high rates the low standard of living of the mass of the population is unlikely to show much change. Transformation in India is slowly gathering speed and it will not be simply of the Indian economy but also of Indian society and the Indian landscape, and much will ultimately depend upon urgency and dedicated endeavour permeating through the whole population.

EGYPT

Egypt provides an outstanding example of an over-populated, under-developed agrarian state passing through a disappointing period of haphazard industrial growth to an awareness of the necessity for full economic planning. It offers an excellent model for the display of the full suite of social, political and economic ills discussed in earlier chapters, and as an example is more manageable in scale, numbers and complexity than India. The fact that the habitable and cultivable land of Egypt, a desert state, is rigidly limited by the amount of Nile water available for irrigation each year, renders Egypt's problems more severe than India's. Almost 97 per cent of Egypt is desert, only 13500 sq. miles are habitable and the cultivable area is only 8500 sq. miles; the population is thirty-six million and now increasing at a rate of 2·6 per cent per annum. With the amount of farmland so limited and the demand for it so great, prices and rents soared as the years passed (until the Revolutionary government established some controls) delineating the typical two-class society of under-developed countries – the small group of exceedingly rich and usually absentee landowners and the great mass of poverty-stricken peasantry. The maldistribution of landownership was such that in 1950 a mere 6 per cent of landowners possessed two-thirds of Egypt's farmland; the remaining third was shared between two and a half million peasants, the majority of their holdings being of less than half an acre. Thus in addition to a growing mass of landless peasantry many of the smallest landowners also needed to seek work on the larger holdings and the over-abundance of agricultural labour kept wages at a level barely sufficient for the most primitive necessities of life, a situation that has barely changed during the past decade.

The degree of under-employment is very high: probably agricultural production would not fall even if a farming population of nearly ten million were withdrawn from rural Egypt. It is this very great excess of rural population that depresses living standards and preserves the status quo in farm practice and efficiency. The unequal division of wealth and the enormous number who shared the lesser portion resulted in pathetically low standards of living and negligible standards of health and education among the bulk of the population. Throughout the 1930s the Egyptian economy stagnated; the corrupt and inefficient administration closed its eyes to the worsening conditions of the mass of the people as population increase outpaced the slow development of the economy and diminishing returns steadily eroded the living standards of the rural masses. Indeed, it was the ruling class who profited most by the forcing up of land rents and the cheapening of labour.

Economic and demographic conditions in Egypt up to 1952 have been discussed in some detail elsewhere;[7] as a background it is sufficient here to underline the attraction and absorption of investment in land rather than in utilities and industry which offered lower and less-assured returns, and the dependence of the entire economy upon the cotton crop. Cotton is Egypt's sole major export and accounted for over four-fifths of total value of exports between the wars and for 60–70 per cent of their total value in the first decade after the last war.

The limited industrial development in Egypt between the wars received a considerable fillip in 1930 when graduated tariffs were imposed on imports of raw materials, semi-finished and fully manufactured goods. This stimulated some fresh industrial promotion but the lack of capital, the poor quality of the labour and the very limited home market were heavy restraints. The period of the Second World War saw the virtual cessation of imported manufactures and local industry found itself in command of the home market. A boom period followed, but many of the less efficient establishments went out of business in the early post-war years with the return of competition from better quality and cheaper imported goods. Investment once more swung to land and agriculture. By 1952 industry contributed barely 10 per cent of the national income. The principal industries up to that time were those customary in under-developed agrarian countries and were based almost entirely upon indigenous raw materials, mainly of agricultural origin. The textile industry (using cotton, wool and rayon) took first place and had grown to satisfy almost the entire home demand; among the food industries were sugar refining, oilseed crushing, milling, brewing, fruit and vegetable preserving and canning; certain chemicals were manufactured, and also boots, shoes and leather goods, glass, cement, tobacco and cigarettes. The narrowness of the home market (being insufficient to sustain competition between several large firms) was overcome in some industries by the development of monopoly and cartel features. Sugar, cement and glass are examples of the former; textiles, cigarettes and brewing the latter.[8]

The structure of Egyptian industry in the period immediately after the Second World War revealed a multitude of small concerns of workshop rather than factory character: 92 per cent of industrial establishments in 1948 each employed less than five workers and 80 per cent of firms had a capital investment of less than £E100 (£E then = £1 0s 6d sterling). At the other end of the scale, and with little in between, were a few really large firms of substantial financial and productive power (particularly in the textile, sugar and cement industries). These few large fully mechanized establishments were responsible for the bulk of the country's industrial output. Such a pattern is not unusual in developing countries (India shows a similar pattern); small firms are likely to proliferate where capital is scarce and labour abundant, for they make small demands upon investment and reduce the handicaps stemming from a lack of managerial ability and limited knowledge of accounting, costing and statistical techniques. The growth of a few large firms was dependent upon monopoly or cartel features and on the fact that capital was more readily available to large firms than to small. Tariff protection, by reducing competition, furthered monopolistic development and helped to perpetuate inefficient high cost production; this in turn limited still further the small home market.

In 1944 the first Census of Industrial Production in Egypt permitted an analysis of manufacturing costs and revealed that salaries and wages made up only 12·6 per cent of industrial expenses, but raw materials accounted for 79·8 per cent, a situation very different in developed countries.[9] Most of the raw materials were home-produced and their high cost reflected low labour productivity, manual rather than mechanical methods of extraction or production, high transport costs, wasteful and uneconomic use in the factories. Costs of production were also inflated by weakness in management revealed by lack of foresight, exaggerated scales of expenditure and poor factory organization. Management claimed disproportionately high salary scales, and widespread nepotism and favouritism permeating the whole of Egyptian industry resulted in uneconomic staffing with a high proportion of administrative and clerical grades. The textile industry classed 19·9 per cent of its employees as administrative, technical or clerical staff; in Britain the proportion was 6·3 per cent. For the leather industry the comparative proportions were 20 per cent and 10 per cent.

This industrial development – haphazard, unco-ordinated, expensive – made but a minor contribution to the national income and to the depressing population situation. After twenty years of protection it offered employment to barely one-tenth of the working population and had little effect upon the lives of the rural masses. The government did little to stimulate industry during the post-war years. It was responsible for the enforcement of an 'Egyptianization' policy after 1947, whereby 75 per cent of employees and 90 per cent of workmen in joint-stock companies had to be Egyptians, while 51 per cent of the capital of all new joint-stock companies had to be owned by Egyptians. These measures were contrary to Egypt's real industrial interests; they aggravated the lack of technical, skilled and foremen staff by the withdrawal of foreigners and discouraged potential foreign investors. Nationalist feeling also led to changes in mining law, making operations and prospecting prohibitive for a number of foreign oil firms who withdrew or reduced their capital outlays.[10]

The subjection of the Egyptian economy to the vagaries of international cotton markets was amply demonstrated with the Korean war boom and the subsequent slump, 1950–2. Prices and exports rose during the boom but little of the heavy profit was reinvested, much went on luxury imports and there were substantial trade deficits. Manipulation on the Alexandria market priced Egyptian cotton out of the contracting world market in 1952 and there followed a severe economic crisis with the country upon the verge of bankruptcy. The almost bloodless revolution of July 1952 was the act of a group of young army officers sickened by the corruption, bribery, favouritism and general ineptitude of the ruling class and the unappetizing spectacle of Egypt's decadent political and social life. They were almost unprepared for the sweeping success of their coup; they had virtually no political nor economic plans and found themselves coping with government on an *ad hoc* basis. To this, and the sheer size and state of the Augean stables they sought to cleanse, we must attribute the slow progress of the economy during the next few years.

It was suggested earlier that little short of revolution might seem likely to bring about social, political and economic upheaval necessary to free feudal-type agrarian economies from the domination of the landowning ruling class. The Egyptian revolution served such a purpose, but was less drastic than if it had been a rising of the peasantry and working classes rather than of the middle class. A Land Reform Act was one of the first measures of the new government, its object being to strike at the 'feudal mentality' enslaving the peasantry and to curb the power of the large landowners. The maximum-sized individual holding was restricted to 200 feddans plus 50 feddans for each of two children (1 feddan = 1·038 acres); excess land was expropriated and redistributed in plots of up to *c.* 5 feddans among the peasantry. This was indeed a moderate measure, for property of 300 feddans was worth £8000–£9000 a year to its owner. In all, some 2000 landowners were first affected. Subsequently, amendments have reduced family holdings to a maximum of 100 feddans, and rather more than 15 per cent of Egypt's farmland has been redistributed, but thousands of peasant families are still landless. This merely underlines the lack of cultivable land in Egypt, for even if all farmland were divided into small peasant plots, there would still be landless peasantry. The transference of the land, spread over a number of years, was facilitated by the prevailing habit of the large landowners to rent out most of their land rather than farm it themselves; in fact, their large estates were farmed in small plots using a plenitude of labour and the change of title deed did little to upset the pattern of agricultural production. Co-operative societies were successfully established to replace the landlord, as a provider of finance, seeds, fertilizer and marketing. A further major feature of the act, affecting two-thirds of Egypt's farmland, was the fixing of annual land rentals at seven times the value of the low Land Tax assessments of the 1940s (a case of the biter bit, for the low rates of tax emanated from self-interest of the rulers). This reduced rents by at least a half and was a further measure to redistribute income in favour of the peasantry. Another revolutionary measure was that holdings could not be divided on the death of the owner. Descendants must decide as to the inheritance of the land; thus it was hoped to stem the fragmentation of holdings, a system prevalent under the Moslem law of equal inheritance.

In 1951 over a fifth of rural income went to the large landowners, in 1956 only one-tenth; the total increase in the income of the small landowners was about £E30 million, representing only a small amount per family but vital to their well-being. Practically the whole of the increase was spent on food; the position when Egyptian-made manufactures can be bought by the mass of the people is still some way off. Unfortunately much less has been done for the landless labourers, comprising nearly two-fifths of Egypt's rural population. Their lot has not improved and with rising prices may well have worsened. Land reform eased the demand for labour on large estates and economic conditions undermined attempts at establishing a minimum daily wage. Agricultural output has risen, thanks to incentives to better farming provided by the spread of co-operatives and the new ownership policy.

Measures in the industrial field after the revolution were less prompt and less sure. The pressing population problem requires greater production from agriculture, more land to be reclaimed from the desert and delta and the provision of water for its irrigation, and greater output from industry. Land reform was aimed at improving agriculture and shifting the attraction for investment from land to industry; the highly expensive and grandiose High Dam Scheme came to be the corner-stone of the government's plan to increase the cultivated area; but co-ordination of industrial development was delayed. Efforts were made to ease restrictions on foreign capital, particularly in the oil and mining industries, and certain measures such as the exemption of new industries from taxes on profits for seven years, were passed. These measures were insufficient to make industry particularly attractive to investment, for the market for home manufactures remained stagnant. By 1954 the prestige of the Revolutionary government was becoming linked with economic development, but neither an overall plan nor investment priorities had yet been formulated. The principal difficulty was finance: precise figures of national income are lacking but estimates by the National Bank of Egypt for 1954 suggest net capital formation at £E54 million per annum or about 6 per cent of the national income and in 1955 at £E68 million, or 9 per cent of the national income.[11] With the high rate of population increase this latter rate was sufficient to maintain existing standards of living, but gave little margin for financing large-scale development. Nevertheless a number of major and somewhat ostentatious projects were begun; an agreement to establish an iron and steel industry was signed with a West German firm, the government oil refinery at Suez was enlarged, plans for a big fertilizer plant at Aswan were prepared. Public loans and funds confiscated from the royal estate financed the earlier measures, then came a period of assistance from the United States of America followed, after the Suez crisis, by aid from the Eastern Bloc.

Gradually the revolutionary government, stifling all opposition, extended its power and after the Suez crisis, when it emerged triumphant, secured a firm grip on the whole economy by its sequestration of foreign business, banks and insurance in addition to securing the revenue of the Canal itself. A new and vociferous wave of nationalism had surged over the country supporting these 'Egyptianization' measures, which effectively ousted foreign commercial influence and made the government, through its Economic Development Organization, a major owner and controller of capital. Even at this stage no national economic plan has been prepared to point the way to the 'New Industrial Egypt' listed as one of the aims of the Revolution.

A hasty industrial plan, little more than a list of projects, appeared the next year, 1957. In many respects it was quite unrealistic and demonstrates miscalculations even more glaring than those of India's second Plan. The plan aimed at raising the industrial sector of the national income from £E100 million to £E184 million in five years, assuming that the rest of the economy would expand at the rate of 2 per cent per annum and that the per capita income should double in twenty years. Manufacturing industries were to need £E181 million while the mining and oil industries and training schemes took a further £E70 million. Thus about £E50 millon in new investment would be required each year – an amount about equal to the total annual saving of the nation and from which provision had to be made also for agriculture, communications, social service investment, and so on. The means of obtaining the necessary capital, especially the estimated £E123 million of foreign currency, were not made clear.[12] Even more optimism is to be found in the assumption that up to 500000 new jobs would be created in secondary and tertiary occupations – this when most existing Egyptian industry was on single-shift working and hard pressed to find markets. Where the extensive markets for the spate of new manufactures were to be found was not specified, but it was not likely to be self-engendered for even if all the new jobs were created, practically the whole income of the workers would need to go on food, housing and transport: their capacity to buy industrial products would be small. For want of a better plan this was first accepted by the government and a four-year credit of about £E60 million was obtained from the USSR. The need for a comprehensive development plan for the whole economy was becoming apparent and this was put in hand in 1958 with the industrial 'plan' undergoing modification to fit within it. The first Five Year Plan was eventually announced in July 1960.

Egyptian industrial production had shown substantial, if uneven, growth during the 1950s, a good deal of the expansion occurring near the end of the period when infra-structure investment, especially in power and transport, was beginning to mature. A substantial renewal and renovation of the railway system, a considerable road construction and improvement programme, and improvement of inland river navigation representing some £E60 million investment had gradually been completed.

The general advance in Egyptian industrial and mineral production is shown in Table 11. Much of the increased production to 1960 came from established plants and not new creations. Cement works had increased from one to three but during the 1960s marketing the growing output was becoming something of a problem. By 1970 the textile industry (Egypt's largest single industry) was processing 40 per cent of the domestic cotton crop and exporting 30 per cent of its yarn production and 20 per cent of its textile manufactures. A valuable post-war industry has been the manufacture of fertilizers, urgently needed by Egyptian agriculture. Some 400000 tons of calcium nitrate and superphosphate are produced by a plant at Suez, but all agricultural needs will not be met until this output is

Table 11: *Egypt: industrial and mineral production*

(thousand metric tons)

	1939	1956	1958	1960	1962	1964	1966	1968	1970	1972
Extractive industries										
Crude oil	749	1828	3184	3319	5138	6979	6884	9890	18945	12223
Phosphate	578	615	558	566	602	613	661	1441	716	563
Manganese	120	201	112	286	186	328	186	4	4	2
Iron ore	—	—	178	239	461	447	440	447	451	427
Manufactures										
Cotton yarn	24*	75	88	102	121	131	142	157	164	179
Cotton fabric	20*	52	60	64	79	88	97	102	110	116
Refined sugar	233	287	261	338	333	382	357	380	547	611
Alcohol (thousand litres)	5	15	18	17	16	20	21	27	32	32
Superphosphate	20	170	179	188	164	209	277	306	411	566
Nitrate of lime	—	208	221	257	273	255	261	168	—	
Cement	368	1351	1510	1903	1693	1733	1764	2309	3684	3822
Paper and cardboard	—	32	41	49	88	103	110	116	125	151
Tyres and tubes (thousands)	—	220	289	485	433	614	1136	1832	1566	1824

*Large factories only
SOURCE: Federation of Egyptian Industries.

nearly doubled as a new factory at El Khattara, just north of Aswan, attains full production. This factory, relying on hydro-electric power from the Aswan High Dam, has been built at disproportionate cost. The first estimates of £E47·5 million finally became a total expenditure of £E61 million for the production of 375000 tons of calcium-ammonium nitrate per year.

A similar miscalculation of cost was in the small iron and steel industry established at Helwan, just south of Cairo. There were serious locational problems in establishing this plant, for Egypt possesses no coking coal and the iron ore (about 50 per cent Fe) is obtained from the Eastern Desert, near Aswan. No matter where such a plant were located in Egypt, high transport costs on raw materials would be incurred. The plant at Helwan is 500 miles from the ore fields and over 100 miles from the ports where the coke is imported. Initially the plant was very small, being well below economic size. Original estimates put the cost of the plant at £E17 million. Production was 220000 tons of rolled steel from 265000 tons of pig iron. By 1960, when the plant was working at about half capacity, the construction cost had reached £E28 million. The result of these features is steel produced at costs above world prices. The plant began as little more than a costly prestige project and has never been profitable. Under the second Ten Year Plan the plant is to be expanded to a more economic size, ultimately to produce by 1976 1·2 million tons of steel from 1·5 million tons of pig iron. Other industries that have expanded and now have a firm place include food processing and the manufacture of a wide range of consumer goods, extending from the assembly of lorries and cars to the manufacture of razor blades. The growing chemical industry produces pharmaceuticals, cosmetics, medical supplies and fertilizers, and other manufactures include sanitary ware, glassware, rubber tyres, leather goods, soaps, paints and varnishes.

The geographical distribution of Egyptian industry shows a high concentration on Cairo and Alexandria. These two centres include about two-fifths of the total number of industrial establishments, giving employment to half the industrial labour force. The spread of industry into suburban and adjacent areas of the contiguous provinces of Giza and Qalyubia and Beheira increases the industrial concentration in and around the two cities and now gives employment to 70 per cent of the country's industrial labour force. A change in the coverage of industrial censuses and tabulation after 1950 makes it impossible to make direct comparisons between the most recent and earlier censuses. However, the increasing attractiveness of the two major cities is clear and their rate of population growth (now holding 5·4 and 2·2 million, or one-fifth of the entire population) has been about 5 per cent per annum during the last decade, double the national rate. The agglomeration of industry in and around these cities provides a clear example of the disproportionate pull of the few locations in a developing land where efficient public utilities such as gas, electricity, pure water, telephones, are available with other amenities of civilization and where there is a provision of labour and an effective market. This selective urban growth, while up to a point economically advantageous, is regarded as less desirable on social and political grounds, and attempts are being made to curtail future growth and to spread further new industrial growth into the revivified Canal Zone.

The structure of modern Egyptian industry by size of establishment demonstrates a pattern similar to that of India and one that may be regarded as typical of an industrially young country. The change in census methods, already mentioned, precludes direct comparison with earlier returns but in 1954 some 80 per cent of industrial establishments employed less than ten workers each (Fig. 11). The graph suggests that large-scale industry forms only a tiny proportion of the total number of establishments, but in fact it employs a majority of the labour force and accounts for the bulk of value added. Value added per worker gives a rough measure of economies of scale available to factory rather than workshop concerns, but is also likely to reflect a more efficient use of labour and better management and administration. The attractions and advantages of small-scale establishments where skilled labour, management and capital are relatively scarce are emphasized by their proliferation. Between 1952 and 1954 the vast majority of the new industrial establishments were of small size. The 341 new businesses represented an increase of 10 per cent in total number of establishments, but barely 1·5 per cent more workers were employed. During this period the index of industrial production rose by an estimated 5 per cent. This suggests that even if a very large expansion in industrial production materialized it would be insufficient, from the point of view of employment, to make any real impression upon the growing annual population increase and the population problem as a whole. The industrial census of 1964 recorded 95 per cent of industrial establishments as employing less than ten workers. This suggests a not unexpected proliferation of small concerns, but if

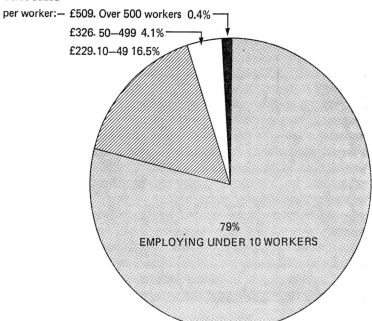

Value added
per worker:– £509. Over 500 workers 0.4%
£326. 50–499 4.1%
£229.10–49 16.5%

79%
EMPLOYING UNDER 10 WORKERS

Fig. 11. Egypt: industrial establishments by numbers employed 1954.

'one worker only' establishments are removed, one discovers that between 1960 and 1964 the proportion of employees in the group of establishments employing two to nine workers fell from 39 per cent to 35 per cent, while those in the group employing 'over twenty persons' rose from 41 per cent to 55 per cent of all workers.

The decade 1950–60 proved a generally disturbed one for the Egyptian economy, being a period of political, social and economic changes, yet by 1960 the mass of the people were little better off than ten years before, indeed many of the poorest were worse off. Small advances had benefited only certain sectors of the population. Benefits to all remained elusive while the annual increase to the population swamped the return from any economic growth. From the industrial structure and small size of the market it is clear that Egypt is still some way from the 'take-off' stage.

The first Five Year Plan, 1960–5 (the first half of a ten-year scheme) aimed at increasing the national income by 40 per cent.[13] It provided for a total investment of £E1577 million, of which 25 per cent was allotted to agriculture and 37 per cent to industry and power. This reflected the special importance the regime has attached to industry, although it recognizes that increase in employment will be less than proportional to the apparent expansion of industry owing to efficient industries using labour-saving equipment. This is also a reflection of gross under-employment in Egyptian agriculture with little prospect of creating more jobs on the land until the farmland area could be expanded, after water from the High Dam became available after 1968. Some £650 million of foreign currency was required, mainly for the industrial sector. The growing population, making heavier demands on existing acres for food, suggested little prospect of increasing agricultural exports, the mainstay of the economy.

The Plan was very ambitious. It was based on a capital:output ratio of 3:1 and aimed at a compound rate of growth of the national income of just over 7 per cent. Many economists felt that this was too optimistic. In fact, at its conclusion in June 1965 a considerable measure of success had been achieved. However, a greater air of realism was then apparent in the government which, instead of launching the country immediately into the second Five Year Plan, called a pause so that the lessons of the first Plan could be studied and the lines of the second Plan modified accordingly.

Investments during the Plan totalled £E1513 million, 96 per cent of the target. The rate of investment to the national income averaged some 20 per cent annually, and this helped to raise the national income during the five years by 37 per cent. This was an annual rate of growth of almost the 7 per cent aimed at. There were, however, also a number of short-falls and shortcomings. Bottlenecks developed where inter-industry requirements had not been co-ordinated; deficiencies in organizational structure became apparent, and there were shortages in technical manpower and a serious shortage of foreign exchange. The general situation was aggravated by the fact that total consumption increased well beyond expectation and, in fact, grew at a rate slightly higher than that of the national income. A major factor responsible was the redistribution of the national income in favour of the poorer people, who spent rather than saved and created an imbalance between supply and demand and caused substantial rises in prices.[14] Above all, there were serious effects from the expanding rate of population increase, which reached almost 2·8 per cent at the end of the period and necessitated a marked increase in imports of grain and other foodstuffs. Excessive imports resulted in a growing deficit in the balance of payments.

At the end of 1965 and in preparation for the second Plan the government faced this situation by raising retail prices on a wide range of goods and slightly raised taxes, in order to withdraw excess purchasing power. Further, investment priority was directed to raising output of existing factories to their maximum capacity rather than to starting new ones, and to give high priority to projects not relying on imported inputs. Finally, a definite policy regarding the population problem was formulated, for with population increase surpassing 2·8 per cent per annum even a high expansion of the national income was not likely to leave much margin for investment and improvement of living standards. An estimate of the per capita income in 1952 was £E30, in 1960 £E38 and in 1969 about £E78. However, official statistics are not entirely reliable and sometimes differ from one ministry to another.

The duration of the second Five Year Plan was extended to seven years and subsequently abandoned: a reflection mainly of external disturbance arising from military assistance to Yemen and the June 1967 war with Israel, the subsequent Israeli occupation of Sinai and the closure of the Suez Canal. Thus, as might be expected, the first Five Year Plan came closer to targets than the second and by 1970, although the planned decline in the relative importance of agriculture was occurring, the shift was less in favour of industry than in the distribution and service sectors.

The second Ten Year Development Plan came into operation in 1973 and is intended to increase industrial production by 10 per cent annually and agricultural production by 5 per cent annually. Included in this plan are the expansion of the Helwan iron and steel plant (mentioned above), the construction with Russian help of an aluminium plant costing £E60 million and of a phosphorus plant costing £E66 million.

To grapple with the country's demographic and economic difficulties the revolutionary government took the most sweeping financial and economic powers, embodied in a series of decrees of July 1961. These measures in themselves constituted a drastic economic revolution, and have had far-reaching social implications. They included the nationalization of banks, insurances and maritime companies, and fifty other companies mainly engaged in basic and heavy industries. Another eighty-three companies were partially nationalized through the state acquiring at least half of each company's capital; this group was mainly engaged in light industries. A third group of 145 companies was also partially nationalized through the government's acquisition of all personal shareholdings in excess of £E10000. These companies mostly comprised textile factories and other light industries mainly owned by a limited number of private individuals or families. A quarter of profits of all companies was to be retained for the workers' benefits; the boards were to conform to a prescribed pattern and directors' fees were to be limited. Income tax was increased on incomes above £E1000, and maximum land-holding for individuals was halved from 200 feddans to 100 feddans, the excess holdings to be distributed among the poor and landless peasantry. In 1963 all cotton exporting and ginning firms and pharmaceutical factories were completely nationalized, as were most of the companies in which the state held a half-share of the capital.

These measures had a number of purposes: one was to enlarge the public sector of the economy to admit greater control of development and ensure the reinvestment of profits. Another was to continue the redistribution of the national income, cutting down even further the number and power of the wealthy, both landowners and industrialists. In a sense these measures signify the failure of the government to enlist the support of an important stratum of Egyptian society in its development planning. That political pressures overcame economic realism is suggested by these decrees being followed, under the guise of overcoming the 'dictatorship of capital', by the confiscation of the property and assets of several hundred persons, mainly from Egypt's commercial middle class, an admixture of Syrians, Greeks, Italians, Lebanese, Jews and Copts. This was particularly serious, in that this class includes the entrepreneurs, businessmen and managers; a class of persons in which Egypt is notably deficient, yet a class essential for the industrial expansion to which the regime is committed. Since 1971 an easement of the rigours of nationalistic and socialist rule has been occurring. Managers have greater freedom in decision-making and an element of competition is favoured. Foreign investment, especially from the West, is encouraged. To some extent the economy is moving out of the hands of the politicians and into those of the technocrats.

After twenty years of revolutionary government the state now controls almost the entire economy and creates as well as nourishes and protects industry, and is its best customer. The foundations of a socialist state have been laid but in terms of economic achievement progress has been slow. The purchasing power of the masses, the real market for manufactures, remains low and industrial development continues at high-cost levels, a situation of mutual exclusion that will persist so long as the rate of population increase remains so high.

Nevertheless the pace of industrial development has been quickening and now equals the share of agriculture (28 per cent) in the gross national product. After the Republic of South Africa Egypt is the most industrialized state in Africa, now having a wide range of food and consumer goods industries. The closing years of the first Ten Year Plan witnessed considerable industrial growth, and this momentum is expected to persist into the second Ten Year Plan as industrial organization improves and expertise increases, as economies of scale become utilized, and as cheaper electric power from the Aswan High Dam brings its benefits. A new spirit is becoming apparent within Egypt and a new image is being presented to the world. The previous coffee-sipping, place-hunting, government-job-seeking attitude of the student population is passing. To work in a factory or on an oilfield is no longer a disgrace or embarrassment. A successful career no longer requires a relative or patron in an influential position. This new sense of purpose and more effective use of human resources offers real hope for the future. However, geographical limitations to Egypt's habitable area are decisive factors affecting her development, rendering the margin for the expansion of agriculture and its productivity relatively small and leaving to industrial development a task seemingly beyond its capacity and potentiality. However, the return of Suez Canal revenues, income from the proposed SUMED oil pipeline between the Gulf of Suez and the Mediterranean near Alexandria, and the exploitation and export of such capital resources as oil, now being discovered in quantity beneath the Western Desert, may substantially change this picture.

Despite governmental determination and optimism and planned heavy investment in the Development Plans, it is difficult to see more than a slight alleviation accruing so long as the population increase is unchecked.

BIBLIOGRAPHICAL REFERENCES

India

1. Sir E. J. Russell, 'India's People and their Food', *Geography* (1952), p. 136.

2. Sir Frank Benham, *Economic Aid to Under-developed Countries* (London, 1961), p. 100.

3. P. N. Dhar, *Small-scale industries in Delhi* (New Delhi, 1958), Part II.

4. W. Kirk, 'The Damodar Valley', *Geog. Review* (1950), pp. 415–43.

5. *The Economist*, 'India Revisited' (1961), p. 343.

6. Government of India: Planning Commission, *Third Five Year Plan* (New Delhi, 1961), p. 455.

Government of India: Planning Commission, *First Five Year Plan* (New Delhi, 1951); *Second Five Year Plan* (New Delhi, 1956); *Fourth Five Year Plan – Resources, Outlays, and Programmes* (New Delhi, 1965).

J. E. Brush, 'The Iron and Steel Industry of India', *Geog. Review* (1952), pp. 36–53.

G. Kuriyan, 'Industrial Development in India since Independence', *Ind. Geog. Jnl.* (1958), pp. 71–8.

J. Orchard, 'Industrialization in Japan, China Mainland, and India', *Annals, Assoc. American Geographers* (1960), pp. 193–215.

W. Clark *et. al.*, *India at Midpassage*, ODI (London, 1965).

J. N. Bhagwati and P. Desai, *India, Planning for Industrialization* (London, 1970).

Egypt

7. A. B. Mountjoy, 'Egypt's Population Problem', *Trans. Inst. Brit. Geographers* (1952), pp. 121–35, and 'Egypt, population and resources' in J. I. Clarke and W. B. Fisher (Eds.), *Populations of the Middle East and North Africa* (London, 1972).

8. A. B. Mountjoy, 'The Development of Industry in Egypt', *Econ. Geog.* (1952), p. 215.

9. Government of Egypt, *Census of Industrial Production, 1944* (Cairo, 1947).

10. A. B. Mountjoy, 'Problems of Industrialization: An Egyptian Example', *Ind. Geog. Jnl., Souvenir Vol.* (1951), p. 22.

11. National Bank of Egypt, *Economic Bulletin* (1956), p. 312.

12. ibid. (1957), pp. 229–31.

13. ibid. (1961), pp. 5–9.

14. ibid. (1965), pp. 243–8.

ibid. (1972), pp. 154–75.

C. Issawi, *Egypt in Revolution* (London, 1963).

United Nations, *Development of Manufacturing Industry in Egypt, Israel, Turkey* (New York, 1958).

B. Hansen and G. A. Marzouk, *Development and economic policy in UAR (Egypt)* (Amsterdam, 1965).

10 Conclusion

In all the examples considered the concept of the wholeness of a country's economy receives ample justification. Industrialization alone can provide no panacea for economic backwardness and poverty for it is but one form of development and its advance is closely related to that of the other sectors of the economy. Infatuation solely with industrialization can bring dire results as the recent history of Argentina shows and, nearer home, the case of Yugoslavia whose agricultural exports withered away with programmes of over-industrialization that ignored the agrarian sector. In 1950 when Yugoslavia suffered famine it was discovered that only 70 per cent of the arable land was being cultivated through lack of incentive because of low price ceilings relative to industrial products and heavy taxation. There is no hope of success for any country if economic advance is one-sided.

The second major conclusion concerns the dynamic but often obstructionist character of demographic factors. Again and again in South-east Asia material gains are cancelled out by unexpectedly high rates of population increase. It seems that Asia can abolish poverty or she can increase her numbers, but it is becoming clear that she cannot do both simultaneously. At the moment too many of the fruits of development are wasted in supporting more people in poverty instead of being used to abolish poverty. The whole problem of development, and particularly the furthering of industrialization, becomes more and more intractable with soaring population totals. These problems beset parts of South-east Asia today but tomorrow will grip Latin America and then Africa. There is no hope of success under these conditions: rates of population must moderate. A population policy to that end must be actively furthered within development plans.

The examples also support the further conclusion that present-day conditions necessitate planned development. The developing countries need to do in a relatively brief period what took several generations in the richer countries that had an early start. The need for planning to mobilize resources and deploy them effectively and economically to the achievement of a definite aim is not an ideological manoeuvre but a common-sense and logical approach to the highly complex parts of the central problem. The plan should be a business prospectus laying down aims, directions, priorities and phasing. But planning that becomes too rigidly nationalistic and bureaucratic loses the support of the people and checks the flow of aid from most external sources.

A fourth conclusion is that there can be no hope of successful industrialization without the establishment of a firm foundation both in social services and public utilities, for the infra-structure concerns human as well as material resources. Here the more adverse influence of environmental factors in extra-temperate climates upon efficiency of labour and costs of basic works must be recognized. The infra-structure requires substantial investment but offers delayed returns.

The example of Hong Kong suggests that something more than doles of capital will be required for successful industrialization. Increasingly 'trade as well as aid' must become a world slogan. Poor countries over-populated in relation to their primary resources must turn to industry for succour; industrialization here cannot be effective if overseas markets are closed to their products. Hong Kong, indeed, may be but a harbinger of things to come. Jeremiahs will not be slow to ask what will happen to world trade if developing countries flood the market with manufactures. The answer is that trade is a two-way process and that both primary and secondary products in the world as a whole must increase together. Growing incomes create greater demand; world trade may well grow faster than ever, for food and raw materials will be urgently needed by the over-populated newly industrializing countries as well as capital goods and more 'difficult' manufactures. Degrees of comparative advantage may play a notable part in determining patterns of specialism, but it is clear that the simpler manufactures will be made increasingly by developing countries.

Another conclusion is that there can be little prospect of successful economic development without goodwill and harmony between all countries. Further it is clear that substantial help from the more fortunate advanced countries has become a *sine qua non*. The call for aid from the developed world, already assuming massive proportions, will continue to increase at an accelerating rate, as the case of India has shown. Here a new and formidable problem is gradually becoming apparent: this is that of the growing indebtedness of Third World countries. According to World Bank estimates the international debts of eighty major developng countries amounted to $33 milliard* in 1964 and had risen to $80 milliard by 1971. Whereas servicing and amortization was $3·5 milliard in 1964 by 1971 it was approaching $8 milliard. Consequently developing countries are now using between one-third and one-half of their foreign exchange earnings merely to service their debts, and this figure is rising sharply. This is a major issue that must be tackled quickly by the world community, particularly since it is coming to be realized that the speed of development is far slower than optimistic forecasts of a decade ago. The idea of 'development in a decade' is giving way to 'development in a half-a-century'. During the first Development Decade the gap between rich and poor nations' incomes became even greater. The rich countries maintained rates of growth of 5–6 per cent a year; the developing countries rates of about 4 per cent. This meant, for example, that each year the United States added to its national income the equivalent of the entire national income of the African continent – some 30 milliard dollars.[1]

Fifteen years ago a group of experts reported to the United Nations that to increase real income per head in under-developed lands by about 2 per cent per annum would need annual capital investment of the order of $10 milliard – a figure that would be substantially higher today.[2] The estimate was particularly high because industrialization was deemed the most urgent problem of many of the countries and the figures were based upon an estimated annual transfer out of agriculture of 1 per cent of the total working population. The capital required for each person absorbed into non-agricultural work was put at $2500. Many disagree with or qualify these figures, but they provide a rough guide-post. Aid to the developing countries in 1971 totalled over $16 milliard, of which nearly one-third came from the United States. This figure has scarcely changed in real money terms over the last few years, although the developed countries have become richer. The United Nations, when the idea of the Development Decade was formulated, hoped for progress towards an annual transfer of 1 per cent of the national incomes of the wealthier countries to the developing world, which, as more development plans gather way, can absorb three to four times the present amount of aid. The developing countries have

---

*One milliard = 1000 million.

become dissatisfied with numerous aspects of the aid system during the 1960s. These poor countries are beginning to recognize that united they have power, in that they control large proportions of natural resources, foodstuffs and raw materials, upon which the economies of the industrialized countries depend. While there are unlikely to be dramatic effects such as those created by the alliance of the oil-producing states, nevertheless a changing relationship between the Third World and its customers is likely to evolve during the 1970s. Changing economic relations between rich and poor are inevitable, with the era of cheap food and cheap commodities passing from the advanced countries, and with a diminution of the 'poor relation' status that so far has been a part of these relationships.

BIBLIOGRAPHICAL REFERENCES

1. B. Ward, 'The Decade of Development – a study in frustration', ODI (London, 1965), p. 5.

2. United Nations, *Measures for the Economic Development of Under-Developed Countries* (New York, 1951), p. 79.

Sir Frank Benham, *Economic Aid to Under-Developed Countries* (London, 1961).

T. Mende, *From Aid to Re-Colonization* (London, 1973).

Index

Accra, 140, 144
Afghanistan, 18, 127
Africa, land ownership, 63, 67;
    population, 32, 35, 37, 47, 69;
    railways, 100–1; roads, 101
Agrarian reform, 154, 170, 178
Agriculture, 19–20, 59, 66–70,
    74–5; disabilities of, 62–4, 65;
    incomes, 60; productivity, 60–2,
    74, 75
Aid, financial, 85–8, 145, 149–50,
    151, 173, 193
Alexandria, 183
Algeria, 18, 20, 112, 128
American Council on Foreign
    Relations, 99
Angola, 18
Ankylostoma, 55
Annaba, 128
Argentine, 18, 58, 100, 118, 150, 191
Asia, population, 32, 34, 35–6, 37,
    39, 66, 67–8, 78, 131, 132; roads,
    101; see also South-East Asia
Assyria, 97
Aswan Dam, 179, 183, 186, 189
Australia, 13, 18, 32, 60, 72, 73,
    84, 99, 158
Austria, 18

Babylon, 47
Balanced growth, 25, 74–5, 88,
    89–90
Bangladesh, 56, 169
Barbados, 18, 66
Bari, 90
Basilicata, 103
Basutoland, 67
Bauchi Plateau, 100

Beira, 101
Belgium, 77
Benelux, 158
Beri-beri, 54
Bessemer process, 23, 152
Bhilai, 166
Bilharzia, 55
Birth control, 37, 43, 46, 51, 56,
    71, 173
Birth rates, 37–9, 41–7, 51–2, 54,
    71, 72, 73
Bokara, 169
Bolivia, 18
Bombay, 104, 171
Brazil, 14, 18, 19, 21, 73, 101, 105,
    111, 112, 114
Brisbane, 99
Britain, 17, 92, 101, 105, 110,
    113–14, 117, 122, 158;
    agricultural productivity, 60;
    economic development, 29,
    76–7, 80–1; occupational
    structure, 60; overseas invest-
    ment, 85; per capita income, 20;
    population, 29, 36, 37, 44, 71,
    78, 79
Bulgaria, 36, 69
Burma, 18, 19, 111

Cairo, 53, 54, 104, 183
Calabar, 147
Calcutta, 104, 166
Canada, 13, 14, 18, 32, 72, 73, 84,
    111
Cantabria, 22
Capital, 22, 23, 29–30, 84–8, 119;
    formation and attraction, 78–88,
    134; per worker, 122, 129, 193;

Capital—*cont.*
  output ratio (capital coefficient),
    48, 50, 81, 82, 102, 164, 168
Capital-intensive industries, 118,
  122, 128–34, 162–3
Carr-Saunders, Sir Alexander, 71
Cement industry, 146–7, 181
Ceylon, *see* Sri Lanka
Chaudhuri, N. C., 100
Chile, 18, 20, 36–7, 73, 148–54
China, 57, 69, 71, 78, 79, 105, 111,
  118; development plans, 161;
  and Hong Kong, 154–7;
  population, 35
Cholera, 54
Clark, Colin, 59
Climate, 96–102, 112
Cocoa Marketing Board, Ghana,
  140
Colombia, 18, 73, 118
Colombo Plan, 75
Concepcion, 150, 151, 153
Copper Belt, Central Africa, 100,
  101; Chile, 150
Costa Rica, 18, 73, 111, 128
Countries, size of, 21–2, 95–6
Cuba, 18, 19

Damodar Valley, 164–5, 166
Death rates, 36–9, 41–7, 56, 71, 73
Debts, 193
Demographic factor, 31, 78, 191
Denmark, 18, 21
Dependency ratio, 48
Development, *see* Economic
  development
Development Decade, United
  Nations, 13, 193
Diminishing returns, 28, 63, 64,
  66, 69
Diseases, 54–6, 96
Disguised unemployment, 67; *see
  also* Population, 'surplus' rural
Djakarta, 104
Dual economy, 136
Durgapur, 166

East Africa, 101, 155

Eastern Europe, farm collectivism,
  63
Economic Development, 14, 20–6,
  27–8, 80–1; and climate, 99;
  and population, 27, 30, 38–9, 50,
  59; and society, 119–20; theory
  of, 24; *see also* Balanced growth
Economics, changes in, 59–60;
  classification, 17; subsistence,
  16, 29, 50
Economics of scale, *see* Scale of
  production
Ecuador, 18
Education, 56–7
Egypt, 18, 54, 55, 58, 68, 69, 70, 71,
  74, 92, 111, 117, 118, 174–89;
  agrarian reform, 91; agricultural
  development, 178–9, 191; capital
  in, 87; development plans, 181,
  183, 185–7, 189; High Dam,
  179, 183, 186, 189; illiteracy, 56;
  industrial development, 131,
  176–8, 179–89; population, 19,
  36, 47, 49, 53, 66, 79, 175, 187
Egypt, Upper, 97
El Khattara, 183
El Salvador, 18
Emigration, 52
Energy, per head, 16; resources,
  105, 109, 110–14
England and Wales, population,
  37–9, 42–3, 44–7, 48
Entrepreneurs, 23, 57, 114–15, 118,
  155, 188
Enugu, 146, 147
Ethiopia, 18, 111
Europe, 13, 110; latifundia, 67;
  population, 32, 35–6, 69, 71;
  see also Eastern Europe *and*
  Western Europe
European Common Market, 158
Expectation of life, 36
Export-Import Bank (Eximbank),
  149–50, 151
Export markets, 23, 91–2, 122–3,
  126

Family limitation, *see* Birth control
Fecundity, 50

Fertility, 43
Fiji, 18
Finland, 18
Food and Agricultural Organization, 25
Foreign exchange, 123
France, 18, 36, 158;
  industrialization, 77
Fryer, D. W., 17

Gabon, 128
Gambia, 18
Germany, industrialization, 77
Ghana, 18, 19, 47, 49, 67, 73, 111,
  122, 139; development plans, 145;
  population, 139–40
Gold Coast, 100, 140–1, 144
Gourou, P., 55
Governmental activity, 57, 86,
  92–3, 102, 123–4, 134–6
Greece, 18, 97
Green Revolution, 170
Guatemala, 18, 73
Guinea, 18, 142
Guyana, 18, 19, 73

Helwan, 183
Hirschman, Professor, 90
Honduras, 18, 73
Hong Kong, 18, 92, 117, 123, 126,
  154–9, 192
Huachipato, 148, 150–4
Hungary, iron and steel, 127–8
Huntington, Ellsworth, 97
Hydro-electricity, 112, 141, 147,
  149, 183, 189

Iceland, 18
Illiteracy, 56, 114, 115, 116, 118
Income, net per capita, 16–19, 58,
  60, 70; net national, 16, 29–30,
  76, 81–2
India, 18, 36, 47, 49, 66, 68, 69, 71,
  73, 76–7, 78, 82, 91, 92, 97, 104,
  111, 131, 161–74; coal
  resources, 111, 166; Five Year
  Plans, 102, 127, 161–74; *1st*, 20,
  50, 81, 90, 164–7; *2nd*, 78, 164,
  172; *3rd*, 163, 164, 167–9, 171,

172, 173; *4th*, 164, 169, 172, 173;
  5th, 87, 172, 174; illiteracy, 56,
  162; income per capita, 20, 162,
  173; minerals, 168–9; nuclear
  power, 114, 171; population, 19,
  36, 161, 167, 168, 172; social
  conditions, 162
Indonesia, 18, 21, 60, 155
Industrialization, 24–5; beginnings
  of, 121; and energy, 110–14;
  objects of, 58; social effects of,
  70–4
Industries, light, 103, 129;
  selection of, 121–6
Infant mortality, 36–7, 42
Infra-structure, 102, 126–7, 181, 192
Interest rates, 87–8, 113, 173
Intermediate technology, 130
International Bank of
  Reconstruction and Development, 84, 149
International Trade, 64, 84, 107,
  192
Investment rates, under-developed
  countries, 50, 81–2
Iran, 18, 115
Iraq, 18, 73, 78
Ireland, 13, 18
Iron and steel, 22, 103, 105, 124,
  127–8, 148, 150–4, 166, 183
Iron ore, 20, 22–3, 101, 106–7, 126,
  128, 151, 162, 168–9
Italy, 18, 69, 90, 95, 103
Ivory Coast, 143–4

Jamaica, 18
Jamshedpur, 166
Japan, 13, 18, 50–1, 74, 92, 111,
  114, 117, 155, 158, 169;
  industrial development, 106;
  investment rates, 83; population,
  35, 36, 51, 73, 79
Java, 71; population, 66, 79
Jinja, 115
Joint Stock Company, 29
Jordan, 18
Juvenility, 47–52

Kainji Dam, 146

Karachi, 104
Kenya, 18, 36, 73, 100, 111, 158
Kumasi, 140
Kuwait, 17, 18
Kuzneto, Professor, 79
Kwashiorkor, 54–5
Kwun Tong, 158

Labour, cheapness, 87–8, 117, 126,
    156; productivity, 99, 106,
    117–18; training, 114, 117, 119,
    126, 171
Labour-intensive industries, 118,
    123, 128–30
Lagos, 100, 146
Land reform, *see* Agrarian reform
Land tenure systems, 20, 66, 67–8,
    154, 175
Latifundia, 67–8
Latin America, 13, 67, 101, 111,
    148–54; population, 19, 34, 35,
    37, 39, 66
Lebanon, 18
Lewis, W. A., 117, 141
Liberia, 18
Libya, 112
Location of industry, 102–3, 171
Lokoja, 146

Malaria, 39, 55
Malawi, 18
Malaya, 19, 20, 55, 128, 155
Malaysia, 18
Mali, 18, 142
Manpower, 114–20
Manufacturing industry, relative
    advantages, 65
Markets, 88–92, 122–3; *see also*
    Export markets
Markham, S. F., 97
Marx, Karl, 30
Mexico, 18, 36, 69, 111
Middle East, 68, 111, 112, 132
'Million' cities, 53
Minerals, export, 20; supply of,
    107–8, 168–9, 182
Misr Bank, 87
Mombasa–Kisumu railway, 100
Morocco, 18, 19, 73, 130

Mozambique, 18, 101
Mukerjee, Professor, 132
Myrdal, G., 89, 95

Natural gas, 112
Nehru, Pandit, 168
Netherlands, 18
New Zealand, 13, 18, 60, 72, 73, 74
Nicaragua, 18
Niger Dam, 146
Nigeria, 18, 100, 101, 122, 139;
    development plans, 143, 145–8;
    oil, 112, 146
Nkalagu, 147
Nkrumah, President, 139, 142
North America, 32, 35, 111
Norway, 18
Nuclear power, 110, 113–14, 171
Nutritional diseases, 54–6

Oil, 17, 19, 84, 86, 105, 106,
    111–12, 146
Oil refineries, 128, 146, 149, 180
Oji River, 147

Pakistan, 18, 111, 112, 115, 127,
    164, 168, 169
Paley Report, 107
Paraguay, 78
Peking, 104
Pellagra, 54
Persian Gulf, 106
Peru, 18, 47, 48, 49
Philippines, 18
Planning strategy, 133
Plantations, 67–8, 89
Poland, 13, 18, 128
Population, 19, 27, 78–9; age
    structures, 41–56; cycle, 37–9,
    43, 47, 72–3; occupational
    structures, 59–62, 161; over-,
    19, 28–9, 66–7, quality of, 54;
    'surplus' rural, 63, 66–7, 68, 69,
    75, 175; theory, 28–30; under-,
    19, 28–9; world growth, 30–7;
    world problem, 27, 69
Port Harcourt, 146
Portugal, 18
Poverty, circle of, 80

Primary activities, 59–61, 63–4
Productivity, 16, 55–6, 61, 90
Protection, 135–6, 162, 177

Queensland, 99

Railways, in Africa, 100–1; in
  Britain, 101; in USA, 102
Raw materials, 64, 105–10, 123,
  124, 126
Rents, 68, 170
Reproduction rate (net), 43, 46
Resources, 21–3, 95–6, 105–12
Rhodesia, 18
Rickets, 54
Rio de Janeiro, 104
Rome, 97
Rostow, W. W., 59, 72, 89, 133
Rourkela, 166
Russell, Sir John, 161
Russia, Tsarist, 83, 92

São Paulo, 104
Sarawak, 73
Scale of production, 117, 130–3,
  163, 184
Schumacher, E. F., 130
Secondary activities, 59–61
Sekondi-Takoradi, 140, 144
Senegal, 18, 111
Share-cropping tenancies, 67
Sierra Leone, 18
Singapore, 18
Smith, Adam, 30, 88
South America *see* Latin America
South-East Asia, 27, 29, 68;
  population, 19, 32, 191
Soviet Union, *see* USSR
Spain, 18, 22–3
Sri Lanka, 19, 36, 39, 51, 73, 111
Steel, *see* Iron and steel
Sudan, 18, 88
Suez Canal, 189
Suez refinery, 180
Sumeria, 97
Sweden, 18, 84, 111
Switzerland, 18, 21, 22, 105–6, 111
Syria, 91
Szczepanik, E., 156

Sztalinvaros, 127

Take-off, 59, 76, 77, 89
Takoradi, 140, 144
Tanzania, 18, 128
Taranto, 90
Taxation policies, 83
Technology, 23
Tema, 140, 144
Terms of trade, 64
Tertiary activities, 59–61
Textiles, 64, 91; Egypt, 117, 176,
  178; Hong Kong, 123, 156, 157
Thailand, 18, 19, 55–6
Third World, 25–6
Townsville, 99
Trade, *see* International trade
Transport, and climate, 100–2;
  costs, 124, 126
Trinidad, 18
Tsuen Wan, 158
Tunisia, 18
Turkey, 18
TVA, 102
Typhus, 54

Uganda, 18, 67, 70, 100, 111, 115,
  158
Unbalanced growth, 90
Under-developed countries,
  characteristics of, 13–14, 19–20
Under-development, reasons for,
  20–3, 66–7
United Africa Company, 89, 148
United Kingdom, 13, 18, 42–3,
  73, 82, 111, 155; labour
  productivity, 123; overseas
  investment, 85; per capita
  income, 17, 21, 31, 36
United Nations, 13, 25, 27, 31, 88,
  136–7, 193
United States, 13, 18, 73, 84, 102,
  105, 107–8, 110, 111, 117, 145,
  151, 155, 158; agricultural
  productivity, 60; mineral
  consumption, 107; national
  income, 193; overseas investment, 86, 91, 180, 193; per
  capita income, 17, 18, 21;

United States—*cont.*
  population, 72
Uranium, 113
Urban advantages, 70–1
Urbanization, 23, 52–4, 70–1, 104
Uruguay, 18
USSR, 13, 18, 24, 32, 57, 63, 83–4,
  126, 181; coal resources, 111
Utilities, 84, 87, 102–4, 122, 123;
  see also Infra-structure

Venezuela, 13, 18, 84, 111
Viscaya, 22
Volta River, hydro-electric scheme,
  141, 144–5

Wales, 95; *see also* England and
  Wales
West Africa, 55, 89, 122, 139, 143,

148; cement industry, 146–7
West Germany, 18
West Indies, 66, 123
Western Europe, 13, 86, 128;
  population, 35–6, 37–9, 42, 47;
  longevity, 47
Women, emancipation, 71–2
Workshop industries, 118
World Bank, *see* International
  Bank of Reconstruction and
  Development
World Health Organization, 25
Worm diseases, 55

Yugoslavia, 58, 70, 191

Zaire, 18, 67
Zambia, 18, 20, 67, 73, 101
Zamindari system, 67–8